HAUNTED
BATTLEFIELDS

Dan Asfar

GHOST HOUSE

Ghost House Books

Distributed by Lone Pine Publishing

10145 – 81 Avenue	1808 – B Street NW, Suite 140
Edmonton, AB T6E 1W9	Auburn, WA 98001
Canada	USA

Website: http://www.ghostbooks.net

National Library of Canada Cataloguing in Publication
Asfar, Dan, 1973–
  Haunted battlefields / Dan Asfar.

  ISBN 1-894877-43-8

  1. Ghosts. 2. Haunted places. 3. Battlefields. I. Title.
  BF1461.A82 2004   133.1   C2004-900160-4

Photo Credits: Every effort has been made to accurately credit photographers. Any errors or omissions should be directed to the publisher for changes in future printings. The photographs and illustrations in this book are reproduced with the kind permission of the following sources: Library of Congress MD, 22-SHARP.V, 4-1 (p. 4, 22), DIG-cwpb-03562 (p. 10), USZ62-100855 (p. 12), HABS, MD, 22-SHARP.V, 9-3 (p. 19), HABS, MD, 22-SHARP.V, 8-A-2 (p. 26), HABS, PA, 46-MER, 1-1 (p. 46), USZC2-2409 (p. 52), USZ62-107919 (p. 70), DIG-cwpb-04090 (p. 78), B8171-7758 (p. 80), DIG-cwpb-00515 (p. 83), USZ62-14298 (p. 99), USZ62-105109 (p. 100), DIG-cwpb-01296 (p. 106), HAER, DEL, 2-WILM.V, 7-2 (p. 126), USZ62-45179 (p. 128), USZC4-3670 (p. 130), USZ62-46972 (p. 163), B813-1685 A-1 (p. 183), HABS, LA, 36-NEWOR, 1-1 (p. 185), HABS, LA, 36-NEWOR, 1-11 (p. 188), USZ62-83277 (p. 204), USZ62-15135 (p. 207); National Archives of Canada C-6643 (p. 110),C-763635 (p. 114); cover of *The Bowmen and Other Legends of the War,* Simpkin, Marshall, Hamilton, Kent & Co. Publishers, 1915 (p. 34).

The stories, folklore and legends in this book are based on the author's collection of sources including individuals whose experiences have led them to believe they have encountered phenomena of some kind or another. They are meant to entertain, and neither the publisher nor the author claims these stories represent fact.

We acknowledge the financial support of the Government of Canada through the Book Publishing Industry Development Program (BPIDP) for our publishing activities.

PC: P5

For Mad Anthony Wayne,
who keeps turning up.

Contents

Acknowledgments

Thanks to those who were crucial to the completion of this book. To Matthew Didier of the Ghosts and Hauntings Research Society, whose historical and supernatural expertise in all things War of 1812 was invaluable. Thanks to the anonymous eyewitnesses whose accounts added so much to the telling of some of these stories. You know who you are; my gratitude for your intelligence and forthrightness. Thanks, as well, to the paranormal storytellers whose works informed more than one tale in this book. Earl Murray's *Ghosts of the Old West,* B. Keith Toney's *Battlefield Ghosts,* James Gay Jones' *Haunted Valley* and Michael Norman and Beth Scott's outstanding achievement, *Haunted Heritage,* were valuable resources. Thanks to the staff at Ghost House Books—namely Shelagh Kubish and Chris Wangler for their deft editing and Carol Woo for sourcing the photos. And kudos to Nancy Foulds and Shane Kennedy for trusting in this book's completion, though an ocean divides us. Finally, thanks to my fellow paranormal raconteurs at Ghost House, whose humor and insight, always welcome, has been instrumental in keeping the ghosts on the page. Thanks.

Introduction

Let's start with the assertion that, in one way or another, every battlefield out there is haunted. Now when I say "haunted" here, I'm not necessarily talking about hauntings of the chain-rattling, tortured-moaning, sheet-fluttering variety. I've visited a few battlefields in my time, and from the cold waters of Omaha Beach, Normandy, to the great big stillness of Gettysburg, Pennsylvania, I can't say I've ever really experienced anything akin to these sorts of specters. In fact, I should probably confess right now in saying that I've never personally witnessed anything close to the supernatural phenomena that fill the following pages—on battlefields or off.

No, these aren't the kind of ghosts that I'm talking about. The "haunted" I'm referring to is something far less dramatic than the phenomena people usually associate with ghosts, than the kind of legends and accounts in the upcoming pages of this book. It is more a vague impression that defies any attempt at concrete definition—a sense that sits somewhere between fascination and unease, curiosity and revulsion.

While not all people visiting the Brandywine Battlefield in southeast Pennsylvania will catch a glimpse of the ghostly Hessian soldiers that are regularly spotted in the area, or, for that matter, spy the galloping apparition of Mad Anthony Wayne, many more will be receptive to the strange tension that hangs over the idyllic Revolutionary War battlefield. What sort of tension, exactly?

It's a hard thing to pin down. Maybe it's an impression that springs from the minds of those visitors who have troubles reconciling the idyllic serenity that reigns today with the terrible violence that occurred there on September 11, 1777. It may arise among those thoughtful visitors who are prone to dwell on matters of mortality—on those who may wonder where, on the battlefield, individual casualties were struck down. Could this visitor be standing on the exact spot where a man met his end over 300 years before? With his last glance, did he look up at the same trees arching above? What were his final thoughts, his regrets? Could he imagine a posterity that would honor his sacrifice? Would he be aware of the historical significance of the battle that had claimed him, or in his final moments, would he be aware only of his own loss?

Whatever their forgotten musings, such men died by the thousands at Brandywine, Gettysburg, Omaha Beach and every other battlefield commemorated across the globe. And whether it is because of the drama of their final moments, the historical significance of their sacrifices or the sheer number of dead, the killing grounds they fought over seem to bear a mysterious gravity to this very day.

Not to worry—the stories in this book are not a meditation on the nature of the prevailing weight that hangs over so many battlefields. These are ghost stories, all based on well-established folktales or else written around eyewitness accounts—all purportedly true. Most of the stories are set on North American battlefields, with the exception of a few British battles that took place on the other side of the Atlantic. And while most of the stories are set on battlefields, not all of them are. Those stories in this book that do not occur on historical contested ground still invariably find their roots in the armed conflict of their day, and more often than not, focus on the aftershocks of tragedies that occurred on the field of battle. Thus, while not every tale deals with the ghosts that linger over battlefields of the past, all the ghosts in this volume are related, in one way or another, with war.

But I've gone on for long enough. There is a bookful of ghostly soldiers, phantom battles and walking, talking casualties from battles long passed. These are the stories of battle that take place after the rifle, cannon and bugle call fall silent—after the bodies are buried and the mourners go home. These are the ghosts that are born from humanity's most brutal behavior, who continue to haunt the ground they fought on…the world they fought for.

The Ghosts of Antietam

The appalling statistics of September 17, 1862, are common knowledge to every Civil War buff. It was on that day, in the fields around the town of Sharpsburg, that over 23,000 American soldiers were killed, wounded or declared missing in action. Widely recognized as the bloodiest day of fighting in American history, casualties at Antietam were nine times greater than American losses at D-Day. More men were killed or wounded in this one Civil War battle than in the War of Independence, War of 1812, Mexican War and Spanish-American War combined. Indeed, there have been few occasions in humanity's history where men have sunk as low as they did at Antietam.

So is it any wonder that Antietam is considered one of the most haunted places in North America? If ghosts truly are born of the trauma of people's last moments, it makes sense for ghosts to be legion in a place where entire legions of men had their lives ripped away from them in the most traumatic ways imaginable. In one instance of the fighting, when Confederate reinforcements surprised a division of Union soldiers advancing through a cornfield, raining rifle fire on their unprotected flank at point-blank range, over 2000 men were killed or wounded in roughly 15 minutes. After the first three hours of fighting, there were over 10,000 casualties scattered over the field of battle.

To many historians, such numbers formed a benchmark for the way men waged war, where the fragility of

A turning point of the Civil War, the Battle of Antietam marked the end of Robert E. Lee's first foray into the North.

human life was laid mercilessly bare in the face of modern technology. If the Civil War is called the world's first truly "modern" conflict, then the casualties at Antietam are the first hint at how horrific these conflicts would be.

On another level, Antietam was a major turning point in the Civil War. Though the battle itself ended in a stale-mate, with neither Confederate nor Union forces able to claim victory, Antietam turned out to be a political windfall for the Union.

Robert E. Lee's Army of Northern Virginia had been running roughshod over the Union army in practically every major engagement before the Sharpsburg battle. They repulsed the Northern invasion of Virginia in the Seven Days' Battles of July that year, only to hand the Union another major defeat at the Second Battle of Bull Run one month later. By the time General Lee had decided to take the war north into Maryland, many believed that the Confederacy might win their independence from the United States, so able did the Confederate army appear compared to the green soldiers and timid command of the North. Yet if a battlefield victory against the indomitable General Lee was too much to ask from a man as cautious as General George McClellan, at the very least President Abraham Lincoln needed to demonstrate to the public that Lee and his Confederate fighting men knew some limits. Antietam was, if nothing else, the limit.

The limit of what? Certainly the limit of Lee's first foray into northern territory. It might also be said that Antietam was the limit of the Confederacy's political momentum, for after the Union army's momentous show of sacrifice at Antietam, no foreign country felt comfortable with any formal recognition of the Confederacy's bid for secession. Both England and France thought twice about lending the South any support after the bloodbath on the Potomac River. And then there was the Emancipation Proclamation. Only after Antietam did Lincoln feel confident enough to end slavery in the United States.

Union General George McLellan oversaw the Army of the Potomac, which tested the mettle of Lee's Confederates.

But there was another sort of limit to the battle. The violence of Antietam was so extreme, the details of the fighting so horrific, that the battle posed grand questions to soldiers in the United States, and perhaps every military man the world over who was paying attention, questions that might still be asked of soldiers today: How much is too much? When does war become butchery? At what point does bravery turn into stupidity and then come back again to sheer heroism? These are all questions that 23,000 Antietam casualties may have answered with their own lives and limbs on September 17, 1862—and perhaps their spirits continue to mull over these questions on the ground where they fell.

Yet on the morning the bloodshed was about to begin, not a single man in Maryland who carried a rifle, saber or revolver dared to ask any of these questions—not out loud, anyway. The roughly 30,000 men of Lee's Army of Northern Virginia were arrayed along the town of Sharpsburg, standing with their backs to the Potomac River against General McClellan's 60,000-man Army of the Potomac. The numbers were stacked against the Confederates, but the onus of the attack was on McClellan, and Lee's soldiers were ready to make the Northerners pay dearly for the foot they gained.

The first shots were fired at about six in the morning, when Major General Joe Hooker's men advanced on General Thomas "Stonewall" Jackson's Confederates, who made up Lee's left flank. Jackson's men lay waiting within the tall stalks of a local farmer's cornfield. When Hooker's men were within range, the Confederates rose out of the cover of the corn and unleashed volley after devastating volley. Hooker responded by pulling his men back and ordering an artillery barrage on the cornfield. It was after the cannons did their deadly work that Hooker made his famous report: "In the time I am writing, every stalk of corn in the northern and greater part of the field was cut as closely as could have been done with a knife, and the slain lay in rows precisely as they had stood in their ranks a few moments before."

Hooker's second advance sent the Southerners reeling back, until their famous general, Stonewall Jackson, rallied them together and ordered the counterattack that drove Hooker nearly back to where he began. This back and forth continued all morning, as attack followed counterattack, which followed counterattack again. It is said that the cornfield switched hands about 15 times before Union General John Sedgwick tried to turn the tide of battle by bringing in his division to assist Hooker. The Confederates were thinking the same thing, however, and the arriving rebel reinforcements got the jump on Sedgwick, hitting his division's flank with sustained fire at point-blank range. Union casualties were awful. It was here that some of the worst killing took place, as Sedgwick lost nearly half his division, roughly 2300 men, in one infamous quarter of an hour.

Meanwhile, while Jackson and Hooker were raising hell on the cornfield, fighting erupted in the center of the Confederate line, where two brigades were positioned along the Sunken Road, an old wagon road that years of use had worn into a shallow trench. At about 10 o'clock in the morning, Brigadier General William French launched a frontal attack on the Sunken Road. The Union soldiers were ordered to march in over an open field to where the two brigades of Confederate men were waiting with loaded rifles.

When the Confederates in the Sunken Road opened fire, the first wave of Federals were decimated. They didn't stand a chance. Parading forward on open ground, they had no cover from the lethal hail of bullets that tore through their ranks, one volley after another. Somehow, the bluecoats found it in themselves to form ranks and fire back. But their enemy was well dug in, and the Northerners' panicked and hasty fire had little effect. French's first wave broke and ran, leaving whooping Confederates behind them.

The Southerners didn't have too much time to celebrate, however. Hot on the heels of the first broken charge was the legendary Brigadier General Thomas Meagher, riding at the head of his Irish Brigade. Meagher's recruiting work back in New York had brought together three regiments composed entirely of Irish immigrants. A proud Irish-American, Meagher was eager to go to war for the Union, and the men under his command would become famous for their incredible bravery on the battlefield. Their assault on the Sunken Road at Antietam remains one of the most storied and celebrated moments of the Civil War.

Unfazed by the broken charge that preceded them, Meagher and his 69th New York marched forward onto the body-strewn field, standing proud under their regimental colors: a brilliant green flag adorned with the gold Celtic harp of their homeland. They had all just received benediction from their battlefield priest, Father Corby, and were ready to defeat the enemy or meet St. Peter trying. On the other side of the field, the Confederates entrenched in the Sunken Road reloaded their rifles and waited.

No officer could ask for more courage from his men, but the 69th faltered at their first taste of lead that day.

The hail of Confederate bullets was so thick that the entire frontline was cut down. They hesitated as their flag fell, the color guard riddled with bullets in the first torrent from the Sunken Road. They stopped, cowed for a moment by the glaring face of death that looked on them from the line of reloading Confederates.

Then General Meagher was there. He had seen his men hesitate, and mortified that his beloved Brigade might turn without firing a single shot at the enemy, galloped up to the front of the line, reminding the Irishmen of their courage by the sheer audacity of his presence—sitting upon his horse shouting orders, completely indifferent to the enemy behind him. "Come on ye Sons of Erin!" he roared to his tentative soldiers, "raise the colors and follow me!"

The next volley was as devastating as the first. Men fell dead left, right and center; General Meagher's horse was shot out from under him and the flag fell again, but this time another soldier grabbed the colors and hoisted them back up before they touched Maryland soil. Meagher picked himself up from under his dead horse, jabbed his saber towards the enemy and let out an ancient Gaelic war cry that steeled the courage of each and every Irishman standing with him. *"Faugh a ballagh!"* came the roar over the Confederate rifle fire, and he was answered by every man behind him.

"Faugh a ballagh!"

It translates roughly as "Clear the Way!" An old war chant that the Irish would have used countless times, no doubt, in their age-old fight against England, but was never before been heard on this side of the Atlantic.

"Faugh a ballagh!" came the soldiers' roar again, sending a tremor of fear through Confederate ranks.

When the next volley came, the Irish Brigade did not slow, but followed their general to the top of a low ridge 100 yards from the Sunken Road, formed ranks, and returned the Confederates' fire. There General Meagher and his 69th regiment remained, matching volley for volley with Lee's sheltered men below. Officers of both sides who surveyed the scene held their breath at the incredible spectacle, as the Irish Brigade stood strong through one barrage after the next, reloaded and returned fire. Undaunted they remained. When the surviving soldiers ran out of ammunition, they picked up the weapons of their dead comrades. Only after there was nothing more to fire at the enemy did Meagher's Irish Brigade retreat, leaving over half their number lying on the battlefield behind them.

The Irish Brigade's charge had hurt the Confederate line, but Lee's men still had a lot of fight in them. They would end up repelling three more charges that day. The same bloody cycle repeated itself, with the Confederate rifles breaking the Union attacks before they got too far. One charge followed another, and it wasn't long before the field in front of the Sunken Road was covered in Union dead. The defenders at the Sunken Road gave up only when two New York regiments were able to occupy a high ridge on the eastern end of the road, from where they were able to rain down a withering fire on the now-exposed Confederates. In a matter of minutes, the recessed road changed from a source of cover to a death trap, as the Southern soldiers scrambled up the sides of the shallow trench while being picked off from above.

More than 300 Confederates surrendered where they stood. After one o'clock in the afternoon, the Sunken Road had been renamed the Bloody Lane.

The last stage of the battle was fought southeast of Sharpsburg, over a 12-foot wide, 125-foot long bridge that spanned Antietam Creek. General Ambrose Burnside had been throwing the full might of his 12,000-man corps against the 450 Georgian sharpshooters since nine o'clock that morning, only to be repulsed time and again. Burnside finally broke through at one o'clock, and by three thirty that afternoon had pushed the Confederate defenders back to the boundaries of Sharpsburg.

If Burnside had captured Sharpsburg, he would have succeeded in cutting off the sole feasible avenue of retreat for Lee's men, who were reeling from the Union attacks that had been coming all day. Indeed, if it were not for General A.P. Hill's timely arrival at the head of 3000 Confederate soldiers from Harpers Ferry, all might have been lost for Lee's Army of Northern Virginia. As it was, General Hill brought his men promptly into action, driving Burnside back to the bridge he had been fighting to cross that morning. The fighting around Burnside Bridge, as it came to be called after the battle, cost the Union 2350 men, the Confederacy 1120.

The fighting ended here, at about five thirty in the afternoon, almost 12 hours after it started. Those 12 hours saw 12,410 Union men and 10,700 Confederates fall— over 23,000 men killed, wounded or missing with no clear victor. It might have ended differently. Lee's army was so crippled that McClellan could have easily destroyed it if he committed the 20,000 fresh soldiers he still had in

Antietam National Battlefield, scene of the worst fighting in American history, is now one of the most haunted places in the United States.

reserve. But the ever-cautious McClellan believed the Confederates to be stronger than they were and didn't have the stomach to keep pushing the offensive. Given the oceans of blood that had been spilled that day, we might hardly blame him.

After the battle was over, both sides were shocked by the carnage they made. Every man who had taken part knew full well that the orgy of death they participated in that day was as terrible as it was historic, and posterity would not soon forget what had been done. Leaders from both sides agreed on an informal truce the next day, and it was with the gravity that some people feel when viewing a great work of art or visiting a holy site that Federal and Confederate soldiers took to the battlefield to remove their dead and wounded.

Though those bodies were removed from the battlefield one day after the battle, there is reason to believe that Antietam's vast communion of death left an indelible impression there, one that lasted even after the bodies were buried and the survivors marched off. A strange and intangible sense of loss continued to linger over the battlefield, even after the Civil War ended and the last of its participants passed on. To this very day, many visitors to Antietam National Battlefield Park will speak of a vague darkness that seems to hang in the air—a vague darkness that, on occasion, has been known to take on vivid and alarming life.

THE PHANTOM RIFLES

Over the years, ghosts have been spotted all over Antietam. More than one visitor walking near the cornfield in the morning has been startled by the distant sound of thousands of rifles being fired. The sound of rifle fire always strikes witnesses as odd: subdued, but too clear to be coming from a great distance, faint, but still loud enough to cause more than one person to start in fear. One witness described it as "coming from everywhere but nowhere, far away and still really close, all at the same time."

Perhaps the sound of rifle fire alone would be enough to arouse only mild curiosity, given the frequency of Civil War reenactments in the area. The sound of the guns, however, is always followed by the pungent smell of gun smoke. Sometimes the odor is said to be so thick that some coughing and sputtering witnesses, convinced they were inhaling lungfuls of burning black smoke, have run away to escape it. Looking back after the first few frightened steps, these Antietam visitors are always shocked to find that the smell is gone, and the air is as clear as it would be anywhere else in the Maryland countryside.

THE LIGHTS ON BURNSIDE BRIDGE

Bizarre phenomena have been reported on the other side of the battlefield as well, around the Burnside Bridge, where the 450 stubborn Georgian sharpshooters stood against General Burnside's 12,000. This is where the lights come out, appearing to visitors who are touring the area at night. According to popular account, they are blue spheres that flicker and bob around the stone bridge, always staying at least 20 yards from any witnesses. While they are known to vanish before anyone who tries to approach them, those who stand and watch long enough claim that the lights are eventually joined by the sound of drums. The drums start faintly, as if coming from a great distance, beating a brisk military cadence. Yet with each passing moment they grow louder, until the night is alive with the staccato beat of a military march. Sometimes the drumbeats last for a

Glowing blue orbs and phantom drumbeats are still seen and heard around Burnside Bridge over Antietam Creek.

quarter of an hour, on other occasions they fall silent after a few minutes, but every time, the lights vanish from sight the moment the drumming stops.

THE GHOSTS OF BLOODY LANE

Accounts of the strange events at the cornfield and Burnside Bridge have made their rounds among supernatural buffs. The battlefield's most talked about phenomenon, however, is neither a distant rifle shot nor flashing lights, but a passionate battle cry that continues to be heard at the center of Lee's old line, along Antietam's Bloody Lane. The most popular telling of the well-established haunting involves a group of sixth graders visiting the battlefield on a field trip. According to this well-documented account, the park guide had taken the group through the entire battlefield before ending the tour at Bloody Lane, where he let the kids walk about on their own, allowing them to absorb the details of the battlefield before returning to discuss their thoughts on what they had seen. And so the kids went out, divided into groups by their teacher and set loose on the ground that had soaked up so much blood in 1862.

This type of tour had been given many times before, and the guide wasn't expecting to hear anything out of the ordinary when the children convened. Most of the time the children in the school groups gave him only a small amount of grudging attention while playing out their schoolyard operas in whispers and giggles. This time would be different.

It began with a single boy belting out the "Fa-la-la-la-la" section of "Deck the Halls," to the gathered group.

"Christmas carols in May?" the guide asked. "What's gotten into you, Jack'?"

"We heard some guys singing it out on the field," the boy answered with a laugh.

"Singing what on the field?" the guide asked. "'Deck the Halls'?"

"You know," the boy answered, laughing again before breaking into another rendition of the carol's chorus, "Fa-la-la-la-la, La-la-la-la."

He didn't get the laugh he had hoped for, and the park guide realized that the rest of the group was quite somber-faced about what they had heard. "They weren't singing," another boy said, obviously irritated by the show his classmate was putting on. "They were kind of shouting it."

At first, the blinking park guide didn't know what to make of what they were saying. "Who was shouting it?" he asked, more to himself than to the students.

"How should we know?" the second boy responded. "You're the one giving the tour." The boy got a round of laughs from his classmates, and his teacher promptly called him on his cheekiness, but the park guide just stood silently, absorbing what the boy had just said.

"Fa-la-la-la-la." He muttered to himself, imitating the mock Christmas carols of the students to himself. One moment passed, and then two. When the revelation came, it came with a cold flood of fear, and the guide turned his back to the students. *"Faugh a ballagh,"* he whispered, trying to come to terms with what the students were saying. The students behind him began to sing "Deck The Halls" again, unaware of the significance of what they had heard. *"Faugh a ballagh,"* he said to himself once more, knowing that it would sound like a "Fa-la-la-la-la" to the unknowing ears of the children. "The battle cry of the Irish Brigade," he muttered. "So the stories are true."

Working in the park, he would have heard the tale of the phantom battle cry before. It was the battlefield's most famous ghost story, reported by countless visitors over the years. It is always heard in the field in front of Bloody Lane, and the words are always the same—*"Faugh a ballagh!"*—the shout of the Irish Brigade who fought with such legendary bravery on that same ground so many years ago. Just like the rifle fire at the cornfield, the battle cry sounds faint, as if coming from a great distance, but is said at the same time to be remarkably clear, clear enough that those who have heard the battle cry have been able to make out the distress in the voices of the men shouting. It is always a throaty and desperate cry—the sound of a thousand men steeling themselves against the fear of an all-but-certain death.

This isn't the only phenomenon that is said to occur around the Bloody Lane. Visitors have also claimed to hear the sound of battle, of gunfire, cannon and the yells of wounded men. Then there are the three sharply dressed Confederate officers who have been spotted strolling down Bloody Lane at sunset. This is the only time they appear, casually walking shoulder to shoulder, casting long shadows over the battlefield at last light. They look so solid, so real, that more than one visitor has mistaken them for Civil War reenactors and shouted out a greeting, only to look on in stunned incomprehension when the figures vanish the moment they open their mouths. The three Confederates' response is the same every time. And while we may never know why these men walk the Sunken Road, and why it is that they never stick around past "hello," they have appeared often enough that a good number of park employees are no longer surprised when witnesses bring them up.

THE PRY HOUSE

The ghosts described above aren't the only haunts associated with the Antietam battlefield. General McClellan used

The natural beauty of the land of the Philip Pry Farm saw much violence during the Battle of Antietam.

the Philip Pry House as his headquarters during the battle. From this sturdy brick house overlooking the battlefield McClellan surveyed the spectacular butchery of Antietam, as runners came and went, dispatching reports and orders to and from each front. The house also served as a hospital for the Federal army's most illustrious wounded. General Joseph Hooker was brought to the house after being wounded in the fight against Stonewall Jackson's men.

The Ghosts of Antietam 27

General Israel Richardson was also carried into the house, struck down by grievous abdominal wounds. Unlike Hooker, Richardson would never leave this makeshift hospital, though he managed to stave off death for over six months before finally succumbing.

Richardson's wife, Frances Richardson, came to the Pry House after the battle to help tend to her husband, and ended up staying by his bedside for the entire half year, watching her husband die a little more every day. We can only imagine how difficult this must have been for the general's wife. Could it have been so difficult that she lost some part of herself in those six months? Left some part of her spirit in the Pry House that she would never be able to reclaim in all her worldly days? This is the most popular explanation for the strange things that go on in the Pry House today, where a spectral vision in a long dress often appears staring out of a second-floor window, from the same room where General Israel Richardson died. And it's believed that it is she who continues to walk up and down the house's creaking stairs, her forlorn spirit still checking on a dying husband who is no longer there.

ST. PAUL EPISCOPAL CHURCH

Of all the supernatural events that occur on and around Antietam, the sounds that come from St. Paul Episcopal Church are the eeriest. Located in Sharpsburg, the church was used as a Confederate field hospital during the fighting. Stretcher bearers began bringing in the wounded soon after the opening shots were fired in the early hours of the morning, and by noon, the church was packed full of the dead and dying. Battlefield medics would have done their best for the wounded under their care, but the brutal techniques and septic conditions of Civil War medicine are well-known, and the mortality rate of the men at St. Paul would have been high.

For many years, certain Sharpsburg residents have been aware of the terrible sounds coming out of St. Paul's. When they've been heard, they've always been heard at night—bloodcurdling shrieks and wails from within the church, loud enough that they are clearly audible to passersby. Indeed, they are loud enough on occasion that people living near the church have heard the cries of the phantom wounded from within their homes.

On these same nights, mysterious flickering lights are seen in the bell tower of the old church. As faint as the lights are, the strobe effect in the tower window is always startling to those who have just heard the screams from within. To this day, no one has been able to provide a solid explanation for these lights without resorting to the church's history as a one-time makeshift hospital—a history that apparently still comes back to haunt it.

In fact, it seems as if the entire battlefield is still within the clutches of its dark history, if the countless testimonials of visitors to Antietam are to be believed. Will the tortured spirits that continue to wage their phantom battle on the fields where they met their demise ever quit the fight? Will the unquantifiable despair of that bloody day ever stop working on those unfortunates who were there? No one can say for certain, leaving nothing but the coming years, decades, perhaps even centuries, to provide the answer.

The Angel of Mons

There are a number of different versions of what happened on the evening of August 23, 1914, when the beleaguered British forces stationed along the Mons Canal in Belgium were finally given the order to fall back. Throughout that day, Sir John French's British Expeditionary Force had stood against the full force of a resolute German army that was determined to make the push through into France. It was there, on the swampy coal fields of industrial Belgium, that British soldiers first met their German adversaries in World War I. And it was there, in the chaos of a battle fully joined, that one of Britain's most lasting and controversial supernatural legends was born.

Occurring in the first month of World War I, the Battle of Mons pitted about 70,000 British Regulars against the 160,000-man German First Army. The British had landed in northern France the previous week and were on their way to join their French allies near the town of Charleroi in Belgium when, on August 22, they ran into advanced scouts of General Alexander von Kluck's enormous First Army. Initially, French was unaware of the size of the approaching German force and prepared his five divisions to take the offensive. Yet incoming intelligence reports throughout the evening of August 22 hinted at the strength of the invaders, and French, thinking better of attack, ordered his men to take defensive positions along the Mons Canal. The British Expeditionary Force had barely finished digging their shallow foxholes around the town of Mons when the sun rose on the morning of August 23, bringing with it a roiling ocean of gray-clad German soldiers.

The First Army occupied the far right flank of the German advance into France, and Von Kluck's orders were to attack any force that stood between it and Paris. So there was very little deliberation about what to do when Von Kluck's senior officers met in the command tent that morning. The order was given for a full frontal assault on the British positions. At 6:30 AM, forward German units were feeling out the British defenses with tentative attacks along the Mons Canal. The British offered stiff resistance, making it known that they did not intend to budge without a fight. So the Germans came, and a fight was what the British got.

By 9 AM, German artillery batteries positioned on a stretch of high ground north of the canal began pounding the British with heavy ordnance. The German infantry assault came soon after, as thousands of men arrayed in dense lines rushed at the canal with set bayonets. That was when the British soldiers dug in on the other side of the waterway opened fire. The men of the 1914 Expeditionary Force were professional soldiers to a man, without a conscript among them, well trained and tested in battle, among the best riflemen in Europe. True to their reputation, the rapid and accurate fire they laid down had a devastating effect on the charging Germans. The first wave slowed, faltered and then stopped.

Yet there would be many more waves to come. The Germans threw themselves at the Mons Canal the entire day, hitting the defenders with line after line of infantry and a continuous hail of artillery. The British refused to budge; even as their casualties mounted, hour by hour, they clung to their positions, keeping up their continuous stream of fire on the attackers—giving far worse than they got. It was a severe and terrible and heroic entrance for the British into the war that would ravage Europe and the world for the next four years.

Of all the units arrayed along the Mons Canal, the 4th Royal Fusiliers and 4th Middlesex battalions absorbed the brunt of the German attack. They were positioned behind a salient on the canal just northeast of the town of Mons and were attacked on all sides throughout the day, kept under a sustained and almost overwhelming pressure. Casualties were bad, but the defenders were resolved to make their stand, staying put under the rain of shells and bullets and maintaining a steady fire on the advancing German columns. But all the skill and bravery in the world wouldn't win the day for the British; there were simply too many Germans.

Hour by hour, the fight on the salient grew more desperate. By around three o'clock the Middlesex and Royal Fusiliers were barely holding on. Despite the brutal casualties the Germans were taking, they were relentless in their attack, hitting the salient with wave after wave, gaining ground an inch at a time. It was at about this time, when the countryside was covered with *feldgrau* as far as the eye could see, that British intelligence discovered exactly what they were up against. Sir John French was promptly informed that his Expeditionary Force was standing before the full might of the German First Army, an army that was dead set on advancing into France.

Recognizing that his men faced impossible odds, French ordered the retreat.

All along the line, the British began pulling back, staging a close fighting withdrawal against the pressing Germans. The two battalions on the canal salient had the toughest time. It was well into dusk when the order to retreat reached the Middlesex and Royal Fusiliers; they were very close to being overrun, still holding their positions by courage and tenacity alone. The Germans were practically on top of them as they pulled out of their foxholes, covered only by a handful of machine gunners ordered to man their positions until the last soldier was out.

What followed then, in the near darkness of that bloody twilight, would become enshrined in the canon of British legend. It happened during the first critical moments of the retreat, when the British rushed from their positions, their backs to their enemies, vulnerable to any attack. The Germans rushed forward as one body, ready to deliver the finishing blow to the stubborn men who had felled so many of their comrades, when the unimaginable occurred: they stopped.

The men providing cover fire from the second line were in the best position to see it. The horde of Germans about to overtake and annihilate the retreating defenders abruptly ceased their advance, each one suddenly still—an army of statues. While they stood motionless, the British vanguard was able to retreat to safety. It was here, at this critical juncture, that the legend of Mons would be written.

By the end of the night, the Battle of Mons was over. The vanguard managed to retreat from the area, and Von

Kluck ordered his men to pause and address their casualties. The British lost about 1600 men during the engagement, the Germans over 5000. Though the British had abandoned the field to the German army, much was made of the British Expeditionary Force's first engagement of the war. There was the usual celebration of patriotic chauvinism. The British lauded the bravery of their soldiers in the face of such hopeless odds, the skill of their men, who, it was said, were able to fire an incredible 15 rounds per minute from their Lee-Enfield rifles with deadly accuracy. But of all the paeans of martial glory the battle produced, nothing caught the public's attention like one British writer's account of the engagement.

Arthur Machen's short book *The Bowmen and Other Legends of the War* was published in September 1914, a few weeks after the Battle of Mons. The book's feature story, "The Bowmen," birthed the Angel of Mons legend, a tale that seized the popular imagination and instantly became accepted as a patriotic, if dubious, matter of fact. Indeed, in the spirit of feverish nationalism that came with the onset of the First World War, few Britons dared to deny the authenticity of Machen's story. Doing so would mean questioning the assumption that God actually was on Britain's side, a doubt tantamount to treason.

"The Bowmen" was a dramatic retelling of the Battle of Mons, bringing readers to the frontlines where British soldiers bade each other gentlemanly farewells in the face of certain death, as others grit their teeth and issued quiet prayers. According to Machen's account, it was one man's silent supplication to God that brought on the miracle at

With his story about the Battle of Mons, Arthur Machen created a lasting, though controversial, legend of the supernatural.

Mons. This unnamed soldier was there when the last men on the salient hauled themselves out of their foxholes and ran for the safety of the rear lines, turning their backs on the Germans, leaving themselves completely vulnerable as they ran. If the Germans would have attacked then, these last soldiers might have all been killed. But that was when Machen's mythical bowmen interceded. They came on the whispered prayer of one soldier, who, looking upon the terrifying sight of the enemy, uttered a prayer in Latin: *Adsit Anglis Sanctus Geogius*—May St. George be present to help the English.

No sooner had the soldier uttered this request than the sky was filled with a great shout and a bright silver light. According to Machen's story, an enormous line of shining bowmen then descended onto the open ground between the Germans and the British. "Array, array, array!" came the call to arms, and the German soldiers stopped in their tracks before the spectral host, frozen in place at the incredible sight. Girded in anachronistic medieval armor, standing tall and solemn in front of the German soldiers, these men were the long-dead archers who fought the French at the battle of Agincourt hundreds of years before.

They spoke in unison, their voices coming together as one mighty shout that thundered over the battlefield.

"St. George for merry England!"

With these words, the line of bowmen each notched an arrow, drew back their bows and fired a single volley at the paralyzed Germans. The glistening sheet of arrows arced over the field and landed among the forward rank of soldiers. Machen might have called it a supernatural artillery barrage, for when the arrows struck, the entire frontline of the German attack fell, dead. Thus the retreating soldiers were able to get away.

There was no way Arthur Machen could have known how popular his story would get. A nationalistic and remarkably credulous British readership anxious about the outbreak of war swallowed the account without question. The implications of the story, that God was on the side of the British and would not let them lose, fit perfectly with the jingoistic spirit of the times. It was soon considered unpatriotic to doubt the veracity of Machen's supernatural bowmen, though no one bothered to ask the suddenly famous author about his sources.

The author must have been pleased by the popularity of his book, but it seems that he was also more than a little alarmed by it. Machen, it turned out, intended his book to be received as a work of fiction, not reported fact, and felt partly responsible for some of the chauvinistic hysteria that gripped Britain in the early months of the First World War. At the peak of his popularity, Machen publicly announced that his story was fiction, that the line of ghostly bowmen was purely a product of his imagination. It was a remarkable confession, with even more remarkable ramifications, spawning the controversy over what happened at Mons.

While Machen's admission gave voice to a strong undercurrent of doubt about the "Bowmen," many Britons did not believe him—indeed, did not want to believe him. Too many found comfort in the idea that supernatural forces were looking over their soldiers on the field of battle, to the point that they refused to believe a denial that came straight from the author.

These diehard believers were given reason for their credulity before long. Eyewitness accounts from soldiers who fought at the Battle of Mons began making their way back home via rumor and correspondence; incredibly, a good number of these stories told of the mysterious phenomenon that lit the night on August 23. Letters dated before "The Bowmen" was published offered varied, though no less spectacular, versions of what occurred when the Middlesex and Royal Fusiliers withdrew from the Mons salient.

One lance corporal who was offering covering fire for his retreating comrades wrote of a light rapidly descending from the sky:

> The light became brighter and brighter and I could see quite distinctly three shapes, one in the center having what looked like outspread wings, the other two were not so large, but were quite plainly distinct from the center one. They appeared to have a long loose-hanging garment of a golden tint, and stood above the German line facing us.

The most common version told by soldiers who fought at Mons involved huge winged figures descending from the sky, and unlike Machen's line of medieval bowmen, the ethereal forms did not attack the Germans but only halted them in their tracks while the British got away.

A chaplain making the rounds in a French military hospital heard a young nurse talking to a group of coworkers about the feverish mutterings of a wounded soldier. The man had been brought in from the Battle of Mons, and since he arrived all he was able to talk about was the angel on the battlefield—wrapped in a luminescent cloud, descending from the sky, hovering between the British and the Germans with giant outstretched wings. The young woman was skeptical, attributing the soldier's rant to a shell-shocked delirium, and laughed sadly as she related the man's story.

According to the chaplain, that was when a nearby colonel, who had heard every word of her story, stepped in to the circle. "Young lady," the officer interrupted, "the thing happened. You need not be so incredulous. I saw it myself." And so another page in the legend of the Angel of Mons was written. The chaplain's tale was published in a number of British papers after he returned from the front, and given the approbation of a priest and a colonel, the Angel of Mons was leant extra credence, over the continued denials of Arthur Machen.

Not that the author's denials mattered anymore. Whether it described a legion of medieval bowmen, a trio of celestial beings or a single shimmering angel, the legend had taken a life of its own and was still a largely unchallenged truth by the end of the war. Yet as the years passed and the First World War receded in time, so too did the extreme nationalism that fed the belief in the battlefield angel wane. While those who stood by the legend during the war did not necessarily disavow it in the coming years, neither was there any reason to defend its veracity with the same ardor. And eventually, the Angel of Mons was filed away with the impossibilities, inhumanities and unimaginable atrocities that occurred in World War I.

That was until March 2001, when the Angel of Mons surfaced once more in the public consciousness. "Brando Inspired by Vision of Mons Angel" read the headline in the *Times.* The "Brando" referred to was none other than actor Marlon Brando, and the "vision" was an unearthed black-and-white film reel that purportedly captured the Angel of Mons descending over the battlefield. The article told the story of a war enthusiast who had purchased two World War I–era film canisters in an antique shop in South Wales. Not knowing what was in the canisters, the man later discovered that he had come into possession of material evidence that proved the Angel of Mons' existence. The article went on to claim that Hollywood director Tony Kaye came to know about the remarkable find and paid out some £350,000 for the footage, which he intended to use as the centerpiece in a feature-length movie about the World War I legend.

So it was that the Angel of Mons became a hot topic in the British media once again, nearly a century after the last British soldier turned and ran from the salient on the Mons Canal. About one year later, a BBC radio documentary featured an interview with a man named Danny Sullivan, the individual who supposedly purchased the film footage at the Welsh antique shop. In a confession incredibly reminiscent of Arthur Machen's admission in 1914, Sullivan declared that he had invented the whole story, that it was a publicity stunt intended to stoke interest in a book he had written about the Angel of Mons a few years before. Yet just as with Machen's confession in World War I, many people refused to believe Sullivan, even though he claimed to be the horse's mouth. Many of those Britons who had gotten excited about the possibility of seeing the Angel of Mons questioned the veracity of Sullivan's claims. Was he the man he claimed to be? And even if he was, who could say what his motives were? For all anyone knew, his confession might have been a ploy to deflate undesirable attention.

The rekindled mystery of Mons continues to be contentious among paranormal enthusiasts to this day, who—as they were when the story of the Angel first surfaced—are divided between believers and skeptics. And yet the question still remains: Were the British retreating at Mons in the evening of August 23, 1915, actually aided by one or more supernatural beings? In this case, how a reader answers that question might depend just as much on the direction of one's national loyalty as it would on faith in a higher power. For, according to the legend, not only did God intercede, but He interceded on behalf of the British against the Germans—a statement that neutral parties and Germans both might wonder at.

The General Wayne Inn

The elderly caretaker worked slowly, lulled into a meditative calm by the silence, the solitude, the gentle repetition of his labor. His thoughts were far away as he dipped mop into bucket, squeezed out the water and pushed the mop over the tiled floor of the General Wayne Inn. As far as he was concerned, the whole town of Merion might have been asleep that night, leaving him alone with his smiling musings. Outside, a dark October night settled over eastern Pennsylvania, where the old Schuylkill River ran under a sharp crescent moon and a brisk wind carried fall's leaves.

Looking after the historic inn was the old man's favorite job. Commissioned to clean the General Wayne Inn every Monday, he quickly learned to look forward to the weekly task. He conceded that his appreciation for the duty probably had something to do with the inn's antiquity. Nearly 300 years old, the General Wayne Inn was one of the first buildings constructed in the region, and when he was alone inside during the quiet of the night, the old janitor might have sworn that the inn was trying to tell its story in muted, almost imperceptible whispers. For the most part, he felt comfortable, strangely at ease within those ancient walls, awed by the General Wayne's incredible age, drawn to its rich history. For instance, he knew how Edgar Allan Poe supposedly penned a few stanzas of "The Raven" while sitting at his favorite table in the common room. The old man also knew a little about the American War of Independence and the story of how

George Washington ate at the inn during the fall of 1777, just before the hard winter at Valley Forge.

The janitor was edified most by the evenings in the historic inn, despite the uneasiness that seized him in the main dining room. An intangible chill belied the quaint comfort of the room with its brass chandeliers, white linen tablecloths and wooden ceiling beams. But if the furnishings of the inn's dining room strove for an impression of warmth, the portrait of the Hessian soldier that hung there emanated an undeniable menace.

The soldier depicted in the painting looked young— young and disdainful. His top lip was curled up into an arrogant smirk, and his cold, disturbingly lifelike eyes shone with barely restrained contempt. Many who noticed the painting in the daytime quipped that the young man mustn't have been too fond of the person who was painting him. Others, noting the care the artist put into portraying the haughty hatefulness of the soldier's features, have remarked that the dislike might have been going the other way. But anyone looking upon the painting at night did not think it was anything to joke about, for then the hatred of the anonymous German mercenary came to life, and wherever one moved in the room, his belligerent stare followed, arrogant, angry and alarmingly animated.

The old man learned to avoid looking at the portrait when his duties took him into the dining room. He could still vividly remember the terror he felt the first time he had become transfixed by the painting, his eyes pulled towards it by something intangible as he was suddenly struck by a dreadful feeling that it was looking back at him, watching him with open disdain. While he was at first entranced by how alive the soldier looked, the janitor's fascination soon turned to fear. Right before his eyes, the man in the painting was breaking free from the pigmented constraints of his portrait, becoming more and more lifelike. Skin formed from canvas as the depth and texture of flesh slowly emerged from the wall. The 18th-century coiffure that had been arranged in static perfection by the artist was given new and disturbing life by errant hairs that suddenly appeared, sticking out, poking from under the soldier's pointed Hessian cap.

And with each passing moment, as the soldier grew evermore lifelike, so too did his look of anger intensify, even as the temperature in the room plummeted. Yet as terrified as he was, the janitor found himself rooted to the floor, unable to look away from the portrait of the soldier. Indeed, only when the soldier looked as if he was about to leap out of the painting was the old man finally motivated to get out of the dining room.

Thus the custodian learned his lesson. Every week after that, he cleaned the dining room quickly, always in a rush to get out as soon as possible, always careful to keep his gaze away from the portrait of the soldier. Each time he walked into the room, his stomach twisted into knots of anxiety and his breathing quickened. All the while, the painting loomed in the periphery of his vision, though he dared not look at it directly. He eventually grew to accept the strange sense of dread that prevailed in the dining room, considering it a small price to pay for the joy he took in the rest of the building.

But that was all about to change on this October night. He felt it the moment he walked in—the sudden chill in the room, sharper than on other nights, the vague sense of malice far more tangible than ever before. He worked quickly, determined to get out of the room fast, when he spied the painting out the corner of his eye, and his blood froze in horror. The soldier was gone. Where the image of the Hessian was once framed, there was only a blank black canvas. It was the same background the soldier had once stood against, but the subject was no longer there. It was as if he had just up and walked out of the painting.

This was the exact thought that had seized the janitor. He spun on his heels, looking frantically for the man that belonged on the wall, certain that the angry Hessian was with him. And there he was. The old man let out a startled yell at the sight of the tall soldier standing in the corner of the dining room. Dressed in the same blue coat, white breeches and pointed gold cap that the painter had captured him in, the Hessian also had the same arrogant sneer spread across his face.

The old man took one step back, and then another. "Please," he said, barely above a whisper. "I'm going."

He took one more cautious step backward before the Hessian came at him, yelling something in German as he strode across the room. The janitor didn't speak German but knew by the terrible glow in the Hessian's eyes that he wasn't friendly. Throwing his mop at the approaching soldier, the janitor turned and ran—out of the dining room, out of the inn, down the block and around the corner, not stopping until his breath was ragged. He did not return to the General Wayne Inn that night.

The next morning, the discarded mop and bucket were the only signs that anything unusual had transpired the night before. The owner of the inn phoned the janitor, asking him why the job had been left half-finished. The old man's voice betrayed his fear. He was still shaken by what happened. "He isn't there anymore?"

"Who isn't here anymore?"

"The soldier."

"What soldier?" The owner was getting exasperated.

"The man in the painting."

"You mean the portrait of the Hessian, in the dining room?"

The owner walked into the dining room and looked at the portrait. It was still there, apparently untouched. The anonymous Hessian soldier stared out of the canvas with the same haughty glare, though it was markedly lifeless in the morning light. He walked back to the telephone. "The painting's still here," he said. "Why? What does the painting have to do with anything?"

"He came out of the painting last night," the old man said.

The owner was incredulous. "You mean the Hessian stepped out of the painting?" He was about to laugh.

That was when the janitor ended the conversation, telling the owner he could find another man to clean up the inn before he hung up the telephone. He never set foot in the General Wayne Inn again.

The story of the frightening portrait wasn't the only strange story to come out of the General Wayne Inn. Indeed, while Hessian ghosts from the American Revolutionary War have been reported all over the northeastern United States, there is no other place where their numbers are so concentrated as in the General Wayne

Revolutionary War soldiers still haunt the General Wayne Inn in Philadelphia.

Inn. Some have claimed that no fewer than eight Hessian soldiers haunt the General Wayne. Who were these Hessians? And why do they appear so often in the ghost lore of the northeast states?

The Hessian soldiers that crossed the Atlantic in 1776 were mercenaries hired by the British, brought overseas to help quash the formation of the United States. They were recruited by the losing side to fight in a conflict they had no vested interest in, among men they weren't even able to communicate with. They were Germans, hired to fight for the British. It was neither their fight nor their land—they were outsiders, in the truest sense of the word.

The War of Independence ran its well-documented course, during which these outsiders did all they could to meet the demands of duty and survival. Their fortunes varied from man to man. Many went back home after the struggle in America was over. Some of the Hessians ended up settling down in the young nation after the fighting. Others succumbed to darker fates—killed on the battle-field and buried in foreign soil. And then there were the other Hessians, those few hapless men doomed to even greater misfortune than their fallen comrades, men whose souls could never overcome the tragic circumstances of their deaths, whose spirits are damned to relive the tragedy of their earthly days far after their days on this earth have expired. Several of these tortured souls are said to be in the General Wayne Inn.

Constructed by a Quaker named Robert Jones in 1704, the inn was built on land purchased from Pennsylvania's founder, William Penn. The establishment was originally called the Wayside Inn, and it quickly became a popular stop for travelers on the Old Lancaster Road, a well-traveled colonial route that linked the bustling city of Philadelphia to the then-outlying town of Radnor. The inn passed from one owner to the next throughout the 18th century, to be renamed the General Wayne Inn in 1795 in honor of Revolutionary War hero and Indian fighter General "Mad" Anthony Wayne. By this time, the inn would have already been haunted.

The General Wayne seems to have acquired most of its ghosts during the Revolutionary War. Situated near more than one battle between British and American forces in the late 1700s, the inn housed men from both sides at different times during the war. And while it has been said that General George Washington acquired a taste for the inn's squirrel stew, it is the Hessian mercenaries who have stayed on there for nearly three centuries.

For the most part, it is believed that the eight colonial-era boarders at the General Wayne are doing fine there. Showing sure signs of being supernatural tipplers, the Hessians have been most often spotted in the inn's bar. Pedestrians walking by late at night long after closing time have seen them. There are always eight; they are situated around the bar, swilling booze, laughing and hollering, their German faintly audible to startled witnesses on the other side of the window. Always, they remain visible until one of the soldiers becomes aware they are being watched, whereupon they all vanish in a blink, leaving no trace that they were ever there.

Yet if the Hessians at the General Wayne seem to be enjoying eternal R & R, there is reason to believe that some of them aren't entirely happy being there. The angry portrait in the dining room wasn't the only one. In their book *Haunted Heritage*, Michael Norman and Beth Scott tell of a psychic who was able to identify one of the lingering spirits in 1976. His name was Mike Benio, and according to Norman and Scott, he had been suffering from restless sleep for some time, thanks to the nightly visits of a solitary specter. Dressed in a colonial-era military uniform, the ghost drifted through Benio's bedroom door at precisely two o'clock each night.

There he would wait until Benio woke from fitful dreams of battlefields blanketed in musket fire and cannon. Staring at the wall above Benio's head, the soldier said the same thing with every visit, speaking English with a heavy German accent, his deep and heavy voice plodding along in a bone-chilling monotone. After introducing himself as Ludwig, the specter embarked on his story. He told Benio that he was killed on one of the Revolutionary War's battlefields near Philadelphia, but instead of receiving a proper soldier's burial, he was interred in the cellar of a roadside inn in Merion. Each night, Ludwig ended his speech with the same demand, that Benio dig his bones from the basement of this inn and bury him in a cemetery.

Some quick research led Benio to the General Wayne Inn, where he promptly received the proprietor's permission to dig in the cellar, as long as he didn't damage the building's foundations. After two days in the basement Benio discovered a small walled-up room that extended underneath the front of the building. Within, he found broken pottery and the skeletal remains of something that looked to be human. Whatever it was, Benio never received another late-night visit from Ludwig after making his find.

On another occasion, the owner of the General Wayne, concerned about the late-night drinking binges that were taking a toll on his liquor stores, called in a psychic named Jean Quinn to investigate. She was able to communicate with a Hessian named Wilhelm who had a story similar to Ludwig's. According to Jean, Wilhelm was also unhappy about they way he was laid to rest. He told Jean that after he was killed in battle, a Patriot officer impressed with his fine uniform and new boots ordered that he be stripped before being buried. Wilhelm never got over the indignity of being buried in his skivvies and informed Jean Quinn that he would continue to haunt the General Wayne Inn until he got his uniform back. Given that no one can say what became of his military garb in the 300 years since, it might be safe to assume that Wilhelm will remain in the General Wayne for a long time.

Yet we might wonder what the Hessians are still doing for fun in the old colonial inn. For in December 1996, tragedy visited the General Wayne. The co-owner of the inn at the time, James Webb, was found dead in the building's third-floor office—shot through the back of the head. The prime suspect was the other co-owner, Guy Sileo, who, as it turned out, committed the murder to cash in on the insurance policy he had taken out on his business partner's life. Sileo was convicted of first-degree murder in August 2001 and is currently serving a life sentence.

The General Wayne closed down for two years following the tragedy and was reopened in 1999 by local property developers. Yet in 2001, the General Wayne was closed down again. As these words are being written, the General Wayne is unoccupied. And so the question begs to be asked. What are the Hessians—those old German casualties of war long expired—doing on this night without the help of a well-stocked bar to pass the hours by?

Hound of the
Hummelbaugh Farm

Gettysburg. There are enough ghost stories about this battle to fill an entire book. Historians, on the other hand, have managed to produce what must be entire libraries of books on this battle alone. Not that they need suffer any derision for this. Gettysburg was, without a doubt, the single most important battle of the Civil War. Often termed the "High Water Mark of the Confederacy" by historians, the momentous battle did indeed mark the limit of General Robert E. Lee's reach into Union territory, as well as the peak of Southern military power in relation to its Northern adversary.

For General Lee and his battle-ready Army of Northern Virginia, Gettysburg was do or die. Knowing full well that the South could never win a war of attrition against the United States, Lee had ordered the June 1863 invasion of Pennsylvania hoping to force just such a battle. If the Confederacy was to win its independence, it would be won on the battlefield, Lee knew, where skilled and battle-hardened Southern soldiers would inflict such losses on their Union foe that public opinion would shift away from President Lincoln's cause.

And so the Army of Northern Virginia spent much of the month of June roaming on Pennsylvanian soil, helping itself to the vast bounty of the lush green state. The Union military brass scrambled to contain the invading army and its cunning general. And so it was that the newly appointed

Confederate General Robert E. Lee planned a bold invasion of Pennsylvania that exploded into the Battle of Gettysburg.

commander of the Army of the Potomac, General George Meade, marched his men to their inevitable collision with fate. The concentration of soldiers, both Union and Confederate, was so heavy in the southern part of central Pennsylvania that a minor engagement for supplies that erupted in the town of Gettysburg quickly escalated into what would become the epic three-day battle that would shape the course of the war.

The largest battle of the Civil War, which pitted General Lee's 75,000 Confederates against Meade's 95,000 Union soldiers, began on July 1, 1863, when advance units of the Army of Northern Virginia marching toward Gettysburg met a smaller force just northwest of town. In a dynamic round of quick, violent clashes, the Confederates drove the Federals south, through the streets of Gettysburg and into the hills south of town. The first day belonged to the South, but this meant very little in the face of the approaching storm.

All through the day and late into the night, Union and Confederate soldiers streamed into the region, regiment after regiment, division after division, so that by the time the sun rose the next day, the full force of both armies were arrayed against one another. Lee's men were positioned in a broad east-west curve that centered on the town of Gettysburg, while Meade's army was dug in south of town into a solid "U" formation, which ran from the far right flank on Culp's Hill southeast of town around to the left flank on Little Round Top, farther to the south.

July 2 was the bloodiest day of the battle, as Lee's generals launched attacks on both Union flanks, aiming to knock Meade's forces off balance and roll the ends of his carefully organized "U" up into a chaotic jumble of defeated units. And so the attacks came. The Confederates initiated a series of engagements that day that would take an honored place in the annals of American military history. Devil's Den, Little Round Top, the Wheatfield, the Peach Orchard, Cemetery Ridge, Culp's Hill…the fighting in each of these areas spawned scores of American legends, as tens of thousands of men met on the field of battle, carrying the fate of the nation with the strength of their arms, the firmness of their hearts and the extent of their courage.

Colonel Joshua Chamberlain and his 20th Maine are still honored in America's military pantheon for their defense of Little Round Top. Major General Daniel Sickles' famous display of gallantry after his leg was blown off by a cannonball still resides in the national memory, nearly 150 years after it happened. The bloodstained uniform of Brigadier General Paul Semmes, who was mortally wounded in the heated fighting for the Wheatfield, is on display at the Museum of the Confederacy in Richmond, Virginia. These men, and many others, all won honors on a day when honor was colored in broad red strokes across green Pennsylvania landscape.

Brigadier General William Barksdale and his Mississippi Brigade occupy one of the highest places among these heroes. Before the war, many may have wondered if old Barksdale had it in him to be a field officer again. A portly ex-Congressman who had served in a Mississippi regiment during the Mexican war, Barksdale was well used to the good life by the time the Civil War began. Yet the strident pro-South, pro-slavery politics he had advocated his entire life left him no choice when the first shots were fired on Fort Sumter. Upon enlistment, he was given a position as state quartermaster general, which he abandoned to join the Confederate army as colonel of the 13th Mississippi soon afterward.

Any doubts that people might have had about Barksdale's ability to lead men into battle would have vanished soon after the 13th Mississippi saw action in the war's eastern theater. Quickly earning a reputation as a fearless officer who was always several paces ahead of his regiment when they charged the enemy, Barksdale so distinguished himself during the Peninsular Campaign of 1862 that he was promoted to Brigadier General. Three other Mississippi regiments joined his 13th Mississippi to form Barksdale's "Mississippi Brigade," as his command came to be known. It was the Mississippi Brigade that was waiting in the cover of the Pitzer Woods on the afternoon of July 2, 1863, as one of Gettysburg's ugliest episodes was unfolding just to the right of them.

Before the two armies converged in the area, no one thought to give local farmer George Rose's 19-acre plot of wheat any kind of title. Why would they? It was a wheat field, like any other. Yet after the brutal fighting of July 2, it would forevermore be known as *the* Wheatfield—a place that no longer had anything to do with George Rose or the growing of wheat, but where over 4000 American casualties fell in some of the worst fighting in the three-day battle. General George Anderson's Georgian Brigade and General Joseph Kershaw's South Carolinians were locked in a desperate battle with Union forces. For over two hours, Barksdale's men were under orders to sit tight as all hell was breaking loose on the Wheatfield.

Barksdale's fiery temperament wasn't at all suited to sitting and waiting, and his displeasure was obvious to any man who saw him that afternoon. The general was a caged animal, pacing back and forth at the front of his brigade, cursing vehemently with every cannon blast that roared over Pitzer Woods. He was under orders to attack the Union position at the Peach Orchard, disable the artillery

battery there and continue as far into Union ranks as possible—but not until he was told. There was probably no
doubt in Barksdale's mind that he and his men would see
action that day; nevertheless, it was often observed that the
sound of combat would drive the general into a battle
fever; his complexion would redden, his eyes would flash
and he would be overcome by rushes of violent energy.

So it was that at around six thirty, when the order to
attack finally came down the line, Barksdale was a dam
ready to burst. Given what the Mississippi Brigade was
about to do, Barksdale's battle fever must have been con-
tagious. "Boys!" the general roared above the din of battle,
"they're finally letting us into this thing!" The soldiers
formed ranks and prepared to advance as Barksdale
swung into the saddle of his big black charger at the front
of his old regiment, the 13th Mississippi. "Now let's show
those Yanks what Mississippi's made of!" Barksdale yelled
over his shoulder. He gave the order to charge, and the
Mississippi Brigade came out of the woods running,
sweeping across the open field towards the Peach Orchard
in a roaring wave.

One eyewitness called it "the most magnificent charge
of the Civil War." It is certainly one of the most famous.
Two Union regiments bravely stood before Barksdale and
his charging brigade but were swept aside by musket ball,
saber and bayonet. Rushing forward in an unstoppable
surge, the Mississippi Brigade smashed everything in its
path, pushing forward past the Peach Orchard and
towards the backbone of the Union line: Cemetery Ridge.
The entire way, Brigadier General Barksdale was riding at
the front of his brigade, urging his men forward with

every plea, commendation and curse in his vocabulary. Barksdale's charge was reinforced by two other brigades, and for a moment, it seemed as if the combined might of the three Confederate brigades together would breach Cemetery Ridge, the backbone of the Union line. If Barksdale had succeeded in occupying Cemetery Ridge, he would have split Meade's entire army in two, which very well could have been the decisive maneuver of the battle, and, perhaps, the Civil War.

There is no doubt that the center section of Cemetery Ridge would have been in Confederate hands if not for the bravery and self-sacrifice of Colonel William Colvill, Jr., and his 1st Minnesota regiment. The only ones left standing between the oncoming Confederates and the ridge, the 262 riflemen in the regiment steeled themselves for the impossible and charged headlong into the flood of gray coats roiling towards the ridge.

The Minnesotans didn't last long against the vastly larger Confederate force. Taking massive casualties in the few minutes they were engaged, the men of the 1st Minnesota did far more than could have been asked of any man and paid dearly for it. Though they kept the Confederates from reaching Cemetery Ridge for only a handful of minutes, it turned out that a handful was enough. Just as what was left of the 1st Minnesota was rallying atop the ridge, a fresh brigade of New Yorkers pushed onto the gap and promptly charged at the Confederates. The 1st Minnesota might have saved the day, but they lost 82 percent of their men through the course of the fighting—a casualty rating unequaled by any other regiment in the war.

As for Barksdale and his men, the arrival of the New York brigade marked the end of their glorious charge. Though they began the rush with all the zeal and ardor in the world, by the time they reached the base of Cemetery Ridge, the Confederate soldiers' will to continue was very nearly spent. They had followed Barksdale deep into enemy lines, sweeping all enemies before them, but now, at the sight of the New Yorkers, they balked. General Barksdale, however, was still pushing to keep up the attack. Mounted on his black charger, Barksdale brandished his bloody saber over his head and roared at his men to meet the enemy, before setting spurs towards the oncoming Federals.

Who knows? They might have followed their general forward if a Union bullet hadn't torn through his chest at that moment, sending Barksdale tumbling from his horse. As Barksdale lay gasping for breath, the New Yorkers swept forward, repelling the spent and demoralized Confederates from Cemetery Ridge. Under their fearless general's command, they had come as close as they could to penetrating the Union line, but now it was time for the long run back. In the haste of their retreat, the Mississippi Brigade left their general on the field, where he still lay twitching with a bullet in his lungs when Union stretcher-bearers found him that night.

Barksdale was taken to a Union field hospital that had been set up in the farmhouse of one Jacob Hummelbaugh, where a surgeon was quick to announce that the bullet had inflicted a mortal wound and there was nothing that could be done. Barksdale lived on through the night, coughing and sputtering bloody defiance until he finally gave up the ghost early the next morning. He did not die alone. By the time the general breathed his last breath, a group of spectators had gathered around him, drawn to the famous officer's last moments.

While some Union soldiers stared on in awe or curiosity at the sight of the dead brigadier general, others went to work, stripping the gold lace, buttons and collar insignia from Barksdale's resplendent uniform. He was buried on July 3, as Pickett's Charge was bringing Gettysburg to its roaring conclusion, laid to rest in the yard behind Hummelbaugh's house.

So it was that General William Barksdale did not live to see the headlines plastered across southern newspapers the next day, glorifying the sweeping charge of Barksdale and his Mississippi Brigade. Yet neither did he live to see Pickett's disastrous charge on the well-positioned Union center the next day, the loss of the battle and the ultimate defeat of the Confederacy less than two years later.

After the battle was over, hundreds of Americans made their way to Gettysburg, hoping to find missing loved ones among the over 21,000 wounded or retrieve the remains of fallen friends and relatives. Mrs. Barksdale, the general's widow, was found in this somber pilgrimage, adamant that she be allowed to exhume her husband's body for a proper burial back home in Jackson, Mississippi. She made the journey north to Pennsylvania accompanied by an entourage of mourners and her husband's favorite dog, a loyal hound that had accompanied its master on more than one hunting trip in Mississippi's backwoods.

As difficult as it must have been for Mrs. Barksdale to excavate her husband's freshly buried body, by all accounts it was even more difficult for Barksdale's poor dog. The moment it caught scent of its former master, the dog let out a round of such piteous howls that all present bowed their heads at the sound—an unabashed manifestation of the grief they were trying so hard to contain. Mrs. Barksdale wept openly as Barksdale's canine companion scampered over her husband's grave, manically sniffing the freshly dug soil as it whimpered and whined. When the men with the shovels approached, it lowered itself on its haunches and growled menacingly in a misguided attempt to protect a master that was beyond saving. It backed away only at Mrs. Barksdale's urgent pleas, letting the men begin the grisly work of unearthing the general's remains.

Tense and confused, barely able to contain its anxious whimpering, the animal managed to remain at Mrs. Barksdale's side as the men dug up the grave. But the moment the general's body was lifted from the earth, the dog went berserk. It lunged at the diggers with bared teeth; only the concerted effort of almost everyone on the scene prevented the men who carried Barksdale from being mauled. Some held the hound at bay, tethering it twice over to a stake in the ground, while the others carried Barksdale's remains to a wagon. The wagon departed, and one by one, everyone left for Gettysburg to retire for the evening, until only Mrs. Barksdale and the hound remained at the gravesite.

Her eyes had dried when she finally decided to leave the grave and make her way back into town, but when she turned to go, leash in hand, she found that her husband's hound was determined not to budge. She yanked on the leash, she pleaded and cajoled, she shouted admonishments, but nothing worked. The animal kept itself planted firmly on its master's grave, determined not to move. It was well into dusk when Mrs. Barksdale decided that she needed to get some rest. Deciding that the dog would be more willing to join her after it spent a night alone, she staked the leash into the ground next to her husband's grave and got into the last remaining wagon, ordering the driver to take her to town.

That night, the hound's pathetic howls were heard for miles around. It began the moment Mrs. Barksdale's wagon was out of sight and did not quit until the morning sun rose over the abandoned gravesite. Mrs. Barksdale arrived soon after, trying once more to get the dog to come with her. Again, she pleaded, cajoled and admonished, but the dog wasn't going anywhere. Mrs. Barksdale finally let the dog get its way. If this is where it wanted to be, then so be it. She untied the leash and briskly walked away, intentionally keeping herself from looking back at her husband's favorite dog. While her thoughts would have been clouded by grief, on some level Mrs. Barksdale probably assumed that someone would eventually take the dog in. How could she have known that she was initiating one of Gettysburg's most lasting supernatural legends?

No one took the hound in. Not that a number of the locals didn't try. Though no leash kept the hound tied to its master's grave, it never wandered, but lay still all day and howled throughout the night. The first few people to come by intended to adopt the big hound dog for themselves, but the moment they got too close, the dog's rumbling growl and raised hackles made it obvious that General Barksdale's pet wasn't interested in any new masters. The pathetic howls continued, tugging at the conscience of the community, and the locals made an effort to bring food and water to the canine sentinel at the Hummelbaugh farm. They brought gristle, bones, meat and water, laying the sustenance down as close as to the grave as the dog would allow. But the dog was uninterested; the provisions remained untouched. Each day, the hound grew weaker and each night, its sad wails were fainter. In less than a week, the once robust hunting dog was little more than a bundle of skin and bones, and shortly after that, it was dead.

The sad tale of General Barksdale's dog would have quickly been forgotten if not for the bizarre rumor that began to spread through the county a few years later. Local farmers and Gettysburg residents were the first to give the whispered warnings. "If you happen to be traveling on the Taneytown Road at night, stay clear of the Hummelbaugh farm, no matter what kind of noises you hear coming from there."

The noises they were talking about were the spine-tingling howls known to split the silence of peaceful rural nights. They were heard only during the summer, most often during the first week of July, when locals living near the Hummelbaugh farm claimed to hear them almost every night. People who heard the terrible canine baying had little desire to investigate. So loud and horrible was the sound that witnesses swore it couldn't be coming from the throat of any living thing. It didn't take long for word to spread that some unnatural creature was lurking around the Hummelbaugh farm.

The tale grew with each telling. Locals who were said to be too curious for their own good went out to take a look at this purported creature for themselves. The reports they came back with only fed the tale of the nocturnal monster. A handful of eyewitnesses claimed to see an enormous hound in the yard behind the Hummelbaugh farmhouse. The dog was said to be a strange and terrifying sight, slightly transparent and glowing dimly with an eerie blue light. There was no mistaking it for any natural animal that walked under the sun. And it wasn't friendly. Those who made the mistake of taking a tentative step or two towards the beast suddenly found themselves facing a snarling monster that was crouched and ready to pounce.

Of course, locals quickly put the howling hound together with the exhuming of General Barksdale. The incident was still fresh in local memory—the arrival of Mrs. Barksdale with the general's favorite hunting dog, the lone hound that remained behind, vigilant over its former master's grave until death.

Years passed, and the reports of the Hummelbaugh hound eventually became one of the region's established legends. Yet as it turned out, the tale of General Barksdale's dog would make up only one Gettysburg ghost story in a fast-growing canon of supernatural legends centered on the once famously contested ground. The following years saw a proliferation of ghostly tales emerge from the Pennsylvania battlefield. Indeed, for a while it seemed as if every passing month brought more sightings of phantom soldiers, ghostly generals, spectral skirmishes and the like.

The formal history of Gettysburg was soon supplemented by a flood of ghostly anecdotes that came to form a major part of the oral history of the region. And so it was that the tale of the Hummelbaugh hound was crowded out of the vast ghost catalog of Gettysburg ghost stories. Who was too concerned with the ghost of a general's dog when the ghosts of generals themselves were being spotted on the field of battle, issuing their final orders before being cut down by enemy fire?

Over the years, witnesses claimed to see thousands of musket flashes light up the side of Little Round Top for an instant and then vanish. Others would claim to see a spectral rendition of Pickett's fateful charge or the remarkably calm and forthcoming ghost of a solitary Confederate soldier wandering over the boulders of Devil's Den. The sheer number of ghost sightings at Gettysburg has caused many paranormal enthusiasts to dub the battlefield the most haunted place in North America.

It comes as no surprise, then, that the ghost of General Barksdale's poor dog might be forgotten in the crush of Gettysburg haunts that are said to be trapped in the trauma of their final moments. The fact that the hound is no longer seen and is now said to howl only during the first week of July—if it howls at all—has done nothing for its publicity. That being said, any man, woman or child on the Taneytown Road during the first week of July might not look so lightly on the legend of the phantom hound. And any person who happens to be walking alone near the old Hummelbaugh farm after dark might find reason to run when the silent Pennsylvania night is shattered by the terrifying sound of Barksdale's hound baying for its lost master.

Haunted Hat Creek

Though John Stevens (a pseudonym) knows that many people have witnessed strange phenomena at Hat Creek, he's still hesitant to come forward with his true identity when discussing his own experiences there. "No offense," Stevens replies when asked about why he chooses to go by a pseudonym, "but I'm a practicing stockbroker, and there are a lot of people who'd think twice about giving their money to someone who swears he's seen ghosts." Yet while Stevens acknowledges the general skepticism society has towards the supernatural, it dampens none of his own wonder over the subject.

"I wouldn't go so far as to say I'm psychic," Stevens says. He pauses here, considering his next words carefully, continuing in a slower, more measured tone. "But I guess you could say I've been in touch with certain things as long as I can remember."

Certain things?

"When I say 'certain things' that's just my own mealy-mouthed way of talking about ghosts. Now listen, I know that's quite a thing to say, but I've been aware of it my entire life, and only just recently kind of accepted it. It's never been in a Hollywood *Sixth Sense* sort of way," Stevens says, referring to the blockbuster horror-suspense film that featured the child protagonist who famously uttered "I see dead people." "It was never anything like that. But there were lots of times when I was growing up that I just *knew* that there were others, other beings, that other people didn't notice. Ghosts. I was way more in tune with them when I was a kid. Most times, I didn't so much *see* them as I *felt* them. It's hard to explain, and I know it sounds flaky, but they always let me know they were there in ways that I could never easily explain," Stevens says.

"For example, I'll never forget the first time a ghost contacted me. My parents had just bought an old town-house in Bay Ridge, Brooklyn. I was only seven years old, but as soon as we walked into that place I knew that something was up. It was the walls, the hallways, the rooms, the doors: they spoke to me. Not in any way that people speak. I couldn't hear what they were saying with my ears. They went straight to my head. I took one look around and knew all sorts of things I didn't know before. There were pictures, impressions that had nothing to do with me. Even memories that weren't my own."

Stevens pauses for a moment, evidently lost in silent recollection. "The first time I walked into the Bay Ridge property, I think I was doing fine with the whole thing. Of course it's hard to remember exactly what I was feeling. It was such a long time ago. But I'd like to think I was more intrigued than frightened by it. That was until I saw the old man. He scared the living crap out of me."

John had been flooded by all these sensations just by standing at the threshold of the townhouse. The visions got far more powerful when he stepped inside. "The old man spooked me. I felt him coming before I actually saw him, his presence got stronger when I walked up the stairs. He was there when I got to the top. I could see him in the living room, just standing there in the empty room, this old, old man, hunched over and standing there. It actually really spooked me out, and I ran running out of that place bawling my eyes out."

The old man's ghost terrified the young John Stevens at first, but it didn't take long for him go grow accustomed to the presence, and after a while, take a strange comfort in it. "What can I say," Stevens says, "the guy became my buddy. I must've thought it was kind of cool that there was someone in the house that no one else could see. He told me things, or a better way to put it would be *communicated*…he communicated things neither of my parents knew. Like how there was a hidden stash of old coins underneath a loose floorboard in my parents' bedroom."

Stevens kept his relationship with the old man to himself, but every now and then his parents would catch him having a conversation in an empty room or suddenly looking off when a vision would get his attention. "The first few times they asked me who I was talking to, or what I saw, I told them 'It's the old man.' I remember they looked so obviously startled and asked me which old man. I told them 'the old man in the living room.'" Stevens laughs at the recollection. "Well, neither of my parents reacted too well to the old man upstairs thing. My mother was kind of worried, and my dad, well he would get upset, sort of angry…like he thought I was pulling his chain and he didn't think it was funny. I think that was when I decided it'd probably be best to keep the whole thing to myself. Later on, I found out that an old man had owned the place before us. He spent, like, the last 10 years of his life sitting there in that living room. That's where he ended up dying. That's why my parents were so upset about what I saw. Let's face it, who'd be thrilled about having their seven-year-old kid talking about dead old men in the living room?"

From then on, Stevens knew that he had an ability that others didn't, just as he knew that talking about this ability made other people nervous. "I got used to it pretty quick, and I remember it being this thing that was interesting and great and alive. I don't think I was ever too scared. I remember being blown away by all sorts of bizarre impressions when I visited a museum or a really old house. It was a great gift to have."

Stevens speaks in the past tense when referring to his gift because as he grew older, the strength of his visions started to decrease. "The sense diminished gradually— and when I say gradually, I mean over a period of years, so gradual that I barely thought about it when it was happening and didn't miss it too much when it was gone. I was a busy teenager and didn't think about the way things were when I was younger all that much."

Not that Stevens' sense vanished entirely or that his childhood experiences had no effect on how he turned out. "I shouldn't say that my sensitivity to the supernatural was gone. That isn't true. At certain times, in certain places, I'd get hit with that old familiar feeling. The thing is, it would never leave as much of an impression as it did when I was younger. But more than anything else, those things that I saw and felt and heard when I was a kid left me with a deep interest in the past."

So much so that Stevens ended up getting a bachelor's degree in history before shifting his focus to finance. "I'm still a history nut. It's all I read; my shelves are loaded with [history books]. Most of the holidays I take center around a visit to a major museum. I guess on one level or another, I'm looking to recapture the magic of my childhood."

If that's the case, Stevens is enjoying himself doing it. "One of the things I get a real kick out of is historical reenactment," Stevens says. "It's probably one of the most immediate and dramatic ways to immerse yourself in any given time period…not to mention the most fun." Stevens makes a point to participate in at least one historical reenactment a year. "It's always an amazing experience for me. I think most people'd be surprised by how eye-opening a reenactment can be, if you surrender yourself to the experience. When you're dressed up in a military uniform, surrounded by hundreds of people who are dressed the same way, living in the same conditions, reliving a battle on the same ground it was originally fought on—you really get a different kind of understanding for what it must have been to be alive at that time."

Stevens has participated in various historical reenactments, from Revolutionary War battles to the Civil War, considering each of them time well spent. One reenactment, however, turned out to be much more. At the Hat Creek State Historic Site in Nebraska a few years ago, John Stevens had a supernatural encounter far more dramatic than anything he had ever experienced in his childhood.

The historical reenactors camping out on the Nebraska plains were reliving the experiences of General Wesley Merritt's Fifth Cavalry in the summer of 1876. It was the summer that the conflict with the Plains Indians had come to a head. The death of Custer at Little Bighorn in June sent a tremor of fear throughout the nation. George Armstrong Custer, Civil War hero and the nation's favorite son, had

Cheyenne warriors rode out to confront the U.S. Army at Hat Creek, and their ghosts haunt the area still.

suffered complete and utter defeat at the hands of an enemy the Americans looked on with condescension and contempt. Suddenly, it seemed as if the "red savage" might have a fighting chance.

But for the Indians who were languishing on their reservation lands, Little Bighorn was a ray of hope. Cheyenne warriors from the Red Cloud Agency took Little Bighorn as a call to arms—a chance to reclaim their traditional way of life. They mounted a war party and rode north for the Black Hills. The United States Army acted promptly. General Merritt was given orders to intercept the war party and force them back to the reservation.

It was mid-July, roughly a month after Little Bighorn, when the two forces met at Hat Creek in northwest Nebraska. In what was largely a cavalry battle, Merritt's men defeated the outnumbered, outgunned and undernourished Cheyenne. Merritt's chief scout was none other than William F. Cody, the man who would later be known as Buffalo Bill, founder of the legendary Wild West Show. Merritt, Cody and company dealt the Cheyenne a sound defeat and escorted what was left of the war party back to the Red Cloud Reservation. It was one small chapter in the subjugation of the Plains Indians but one that seems to have left a lasting supernatural legacy.

Reports of bizarre happenings at Hat Creek have been circulating for years. Some visitors claim to have caught sight of a group of gaunt Cheyenne warriors riding across the wide plain when the sun touches the horizon. They are visible for only a minute or two before vanishing into nothingness the moment the sun drops from sight. Those who have seen these Cheyenne horsemen are always left with the same impression—a pervasive sense of sadness. Other visitors to Hat Creek claim to have heard footsteps on the prairie grass where no one was walking, while others have reported disembodied voices calling on the wind in a language they do not understand. Yet of all the phenomena that are said to occur at Hat Creek, the most talked about is the green mist. The accounts are always the same as they describe thick, twisting tendrils of green mist that rise out of the grass at night and slowly inch towards terrified witnesses. No one who has seen the green mist at Hat Creek has believed it to be friendly.

John Stevens was familiar with these stories when he went out to relive history at Hat Creek, and he was hoping to witness the spirits of Hat Creek for himself. He ended up getting his wish. "It was the second night we were camped at Hat Creek," Stevens remembers. "There were quite a few of us, and everyone was dressed up in 19th-century cavalry uniforms; we were living on substandard coffee, beans and hardtack. It was awful, but it was also great. There was this sense of communion that hung in the air. It's amazing, the sense of camaraderie you get when you're together with a group of people all wearing the same outfit." Stevens laughs. "You might not know these people from Frank or Henry, but they're dressed the same as you are, so they can't be that bad.

"Anyway," Stevens continues, "for the first two days I was there, I can't say I was feeling anything strange. We were all concentrating on immersing ourselves in the duties and drudgery, just the same as any one of Merritt's boys would have. I think I even forgot about the ghost angle and just got into the spirit of the whole thing." That would change on the second night.

"I can remember it like it was yesterday. It was some-time past midnight when I woke up from this bad dream. Big surprise, I was dreaming about Indians. I can still see the dream with vivid clarity. There was this heavy drum-beat, falling in time with the seconds, getting louder and louder, and there were Sioux and Cheyenne and horses galloping across a flat plain. They were dying by the hundreds, being killed by an enemy that they couldn't see, neither could I. They were being shot to pieces…these strong and proud braves looking as mean as hell on these incredible horses, shot to pieces. It was a horrible mess, and it struck me as such a tragic thing. I woke up sweaty and out of breath and kind of disoriented. It took me a few seconds to remember where I was.

"I'm not sure how long it took me to realize it, but as I was lying there, it started to feel more and more like something wasn't right. There was more going on than the other guys snoring and the tent's white ceiling and the blowing wind. There were *others* out there, outside my tent—others who didn't come out to be part of our historical reenactment. I mean the kind of others that made me feel like I was seven again. I could sense them there. Just like I sensed the old man in Bay Ridge."

Lying in his mock army tent, Stevens wasn't sure what to feel. On one hand, he was terrified at the mystery of what lay outside on the battlefield; on the other, he was buzzing with excitement. "I mean, being out there on the Great Plains, in touch with some part of our national history that you can't get to in the history books. This is heady stuff."

The first footstep might as well have been a trumpet blast for the effect it had on Stevens. Bolting out of bed, he slipped his boots on and headed outside. There was nothing there except the tents and the wind and the stars. The camp was sleeping and the place was quiet, but Stevens wasn't fooled by the tranquility. His hair was standing up on the back of his neck and he was aware of a presence that did not want to be seen and that was standing as still as he was.

And then it was moving, the footfalls running through camp with a light step, barely making a sound on the short grass, just enough for Stevens to make out the direction it was going. His heart jumped, and in the next moment he found himself running in the direction of the footsteps, following the sound as the steps wove their way through the row of tents. He couldn't stop himself. Charged by a decades-long curiosity that demanded to be satisfied, Stevens ran after the invisible presence. "I remember the feeling when I was running after it. I can remember thinking that I'd finally found the thing that would lead me to some sort of answer to all the big questions I'd never asked. I just knew that I couldn't lose whoever, or whatever, was running away. I had to keep up with it."

Stevens kept up with it, never more a few steps behind. It led him out of camp and up the side of a hill on Hat Creek, high enough that he had a wide vista of the grasslands and the tents below. Then the footsteps stopped, leaving Stevens alone in the darkness. "So I was standing there, trying to catch my breath, waiting for something to happen. I still wasn't scared or anything, but a few minutes went by and I started to worry that this was it. All my adult life, waiting for something like this to happen, waiting for an explanation about the things I saw when I was a kid—but there was nothing."

Nothing at first. Stevens stood and waited for what, according to him, "could've been 10 minutes or could've been an hour," and was just about to turn around, when the voices started. "There were a lot of them. They were whispering to each other, speaking a language I couldn't understand, though I knew they were Cheyenne." The voices were in the darkness, all around Stevens. "It felt like I was surrounded, it felt like they were all over the place, camouflaged in the night. I could've been in the middle of a thousand whispering Cheyenne braves. That was when I started to get scared."

Fear suddenly formed in the pit of Stevens' stomach as it dawned on him that these spirits might not be friendly at all, especially to a man dressed in the trappings of their enemy. "I was hit with this strong impression of anger and sadness and hunger. These guys were desperate. They died desperate, without any hope at all. The scene was just immeasurably sad. I had no idea what to do." Awash in a flood of foreign sensations, Stevens found it was all he could do to stand there and absorb the braves' collective anguish. His feet were frozen to the spot.

"I couldn't get myself to do anything. The sensations were so strong I kind of forgot where I was. I can't say how long I would've been standing there if the green mist didn't appear." According to John Stevens, Hat Creek's famous green mist came from the ground—starting as a single coil that shone faintly, rising tentatively from the grass. One tendril, followed by another and yet another, the mist grew before Stevens' eyes, until a churning, billowing fog "the size of two or three horses" stood looming over him.

"I still don't know what to make of that mist," Stevens says today. "Of course I'm assuming that it had something to do with the battle in 1876, but I couldn't get any kind of psychic read on it. Not that I had to. I mean it was obvious with just one look—or that's the way it struck me, anyway. It was mad…really, really angry. I think anger, more than anything, was what gave it life—what made it move. And the second it moved towards me, I was out of there."

Stevens ran down the side of the hill as fast as his legs could take him and did not stop until he was safely back in his tent, where he tossed and turned for the rest of the night. "It was impossible to get back to sleep, and a lot of the guys made comments on how terrible I looked that morning, but I didn't say anything about what I saw. A lot of them would have known the legend of the green mist, but I wasn't about to turn the experience I had the night before into a running joke, which is what would have happened. I guess there's some things you can't really talk about."

This sounds strange, coming from someone who spent the last hour talking about his experience at the Hat Creek battleground. It's obvious that Stevens is a man eager to get the experience off his chest. "I still think about that night at Hat Creek a lot. I've done research into the place since then, and there're quite a few accounts of the green mist out there," Stevens says. "The thing that seems to be missing, though, is the observation that the mist is angry—really angry. A lot of the witnesses I've read up on have been spooked out by it; most run away. But no one has said anything about how terribly angry it was or about how it should probably be left alone."

Ghosts of Fort Stedman

The situation was well beyond desperate when Robert E. Lee gave Major General John B. Gordon the order to break the siege at Petersburg. It was March 1865, and almost everyone, Northerners and Southerners alike, had come to accept the fact that the Civil War was nearing its end. After one year as General-in-Chief of the Union forces, Ulysses Grant had almost accomplished the near total subjugation of the Confederate military. The Confederacy had lost control of the Shenandoah Valley to the United States the previous fall, and in February 1865, the crucial port city of Wilmington, North Carolina, fell to the Union army. On top of everything else, Lee's proud Army of Northern Virginia had been holed up in Petersburg for over nine months, besieged by the numerically superior Army of the Potomac and suffering greatly from starvation and desertion.

But General Lee was not yet ready to concede defeat. As long as the soldiers of the vaunted Army of Northern Virginia were enmeshed within the intricate network of trenches the Union army dug around Petersburg, they were of little use to the Southern cause. But Lee hoped that if his men were able to break out, they would be able to secure more victories against Grant's Union army on the battlefield. The Confederates were outnumbered, outgunned and under-supplied, but Lee's indomitable fighting spirit refused surrender, and so he gave General Gordon the order. "Find a gap in their line that we can

The siege of Petersburg lasted nine months and saw many casualties, both Union and Confederate.

slip our army through. We must break out of this trap within the month, or all is lost."

Gordon returned to Lee three weeks later, telling General Lee that he had found a weakness in the enemy lines. Fort Stedman was located to the right of the Union lines, close to the Appomattox River and a mere 150 yards from the Confederates' trenches. Gordon reasoned that a surprise attack on the fort launched early in the morning might easily lead to the capture of the fort. The Rebels would then fortify the captured fort, securing the breach in the Union line. Gordon and Lee hoped that the attack would pressure Grant to call in soldiers from his extended lines, thereby allowing the rest of the Confederate force to escape from the web of trenches that encased them. General Lee was under no illusions. It was a reckless attack—a frantic, near hopeless attempt to keep the rebellion alive, but as long as there was a chance, no matter how slim, Lee was ready to take it.

Remarkably, the first stage of the attack went quite well. Confederate soldiers had been deserting in droves, so the men stationed at the Union pickets, used to seeing Southern soldiers crossing the battlefield, weren't alarmed when the first group of Confederates emerged from their trenches at 4 AM on the morning of March 25. These men were actually posing as deserters—deserters who were able to bring their rifles along because of a Union mandate that allowed enemy soldiers to surrender their arms for $10 a rifle. Thus the attack on Fort Stedman began without a shot being fired, when a rag-tag contingent of soldiers, who looked hungry enough to be the deserters they were posing as, cowed the Union sentries into surrender by the tips of their bayonets. The assault on Fort Stedman followed, and the garrison there, caught completely by surprise, capitulated almost immediately.

Supporting Confederate units were sent in to exploit the breach, with orders to take over the three artillery batteries that supported Stedman. These promptly fell as well, but that would be the limit of the Confederate push.

Union Major General John Hartranft (front, center) drove Confederates away from Fort Stedman.

Union command reacted quickly. A capable and determined Major General John Hartranft mobilized the IX Corps, and regiments were brought to bear on the breakthrough, even as the Confederate advance floundered. Unsure of where the subsequent Union objectives were located, and not knowing how to navigate the enemy trenches in the darkness of the early morning, the Confederates stalled, just as the Union army began its counterattack in earnest.

General Gordon did not abandon his bridgehead without a fight. He ordered his men to hold on to Fort

Stedman, and for a few hours they did, despite the withering fire of Hartranft's concentrated counterattack. Yet as the enemy massed around him in ever-increasing numbers, Gordon knew that the offensive had failed, and after a brief, bloody fight, he called for the retreat. The Union brass reported the reoccupation of Fort Stedman at 8:15 that morning, roughly four hours after the Confederates launched the attack.

During those four hours about 1000 Union men and anywhere from 2700 to 4000 Confederates were lost. Morale would have been very low among the Southern ranks at this time, and many of Lee's casualties were certainly desertions. Nevertheless, they were losses that General Lee could scarcely afford. Sensing that the foiled offensive had weakened Lee's position, Grant ordered a series of minor attacks all along the Southern line, inching ever closer to Petersburg.

The attack on Fort Stedman was a modest assault, but it would be one of General Lee's last hurrahs. Just over two weeks later, on April 9, Lee laid down his saber and surrendered the Army of Northern Virginia in the town of Appomattox, ushering in the end of the Confederacy and the American Civil War.

Yet according to some, the conflict never truly ended for those men who fought around Fort Stedman in the dying days of the Civil War. Indeed, given the sights and sounds that are reported around the old battlefield to this very day, more than a few Union soldiers have lingered there long after the call of duty expired.

The site of the bloody siege was designated the Petersburg National Battlefield on August 24, 1962. And while it is difficult to know what sort of stories circulated about the place before then, ever since a regular staff was put there, the ghosts of Fort Stedman have become part of the United States' paranormal folklore.

Witnesses who happen to be visiting the battlefield early in the morning have seen the row of ghostly soldiers standing at attention near Fort Stedman, on the same ridge where General Hartranft's soldiers assembled before repulsing the Confederates. The numbers are said to vary. Some onlookers claimed to have seen a handful of men in blue uniforms, while other shocked witnesses have said the ridge was covered in silent men blankly staring forward. But whether it's a single ghostly platoon or an entire phantom legion, the phenomenon always plays out the same.

It is said they stand in utter silence for long moments, staring ahead, dead-eyed, pale, impassive. Whether they are there for one minute or five, their presence is always accompanied by an intangible heaviness that increases with each passing second. And then, suddenly, and without warning, they just vanish. Very few people who catch sight of the ghostly contingent think to speak, think to run or think to do anything else. The overwhelming sensation is a steady and growing sadness, a deep empathy for the men on the hill that comes unexpectedly. Witnesses claim to have been struck by a sudden and terrible understanding of the magnitude of the men's sacrifice. Standing face-to-face with the lost souls of dead soldiers, observers have found themselves confronting the meaning of mortality. Most are left staggered by the experience.

Fort Stedman is now haunted by phantom soldiers, who serve as a poignant reminder of the sacrifices demanded by war.

This isn't the only phenomenon that is said to occur at Fort Stedman. Over the years, a number of park employees have been woken early in the morning, at around six o'clock, to the noise of drums and bugles. A battlefield rally sounds crisp and close, as if an old Civil War regiment was organizing itself just outside. Those who have leapt out to investigate the source of the din are always confronted by the same eerie stillness the moment they open their doors. Where a moment before the morning was a jostling cacophony of drum roll and bugle call, the silence is punctuated only modestly by the trill of a bird or a mild breeze.

And so the phantom soldiers have kept their watch over Fort Stedman. Are they unaware that the conflict is over? Are they angry because their lives were taken just weeks before the Civil War ended? Indeed, if they had lived for only two weeks more, most of them would have been free to live out the rest of their days in relative peace. Or is their appearance intended to be a ghostly memorial? Do they rally morning after morning, year after year, so that their sacrifices will not be forgotten? Whatever the case, General Hartranft's men continue to appear, and be heard, early in the morning, rallying for their final assault on Fort Stedman time and time again.

The Ghost on King's Mountain

Lieutenant Colonel Patrick Ferguson wasn't the kind of man to mince words, put on airs or shirk from action. A rugged pragmatist of shrewd intelligence, the Scottish officer stood apart in many ways from much of the British military brass, who were steeped in the affected civility and traditionalism they were so famous for. Thus this officer of the British Crown had a strange sort of kinship with the American mountain men in the southern colonies who, during the War of Independence, would become his mortal enemies.

The year was 1780. The place South Carolina. By this time, the commander of the British Forces in North America, Sir Henry Clinton, was forced to concede that the fight for control of the colonies was going badly in the North, where rebel Patriot sympathies were running high. Shifting the focus of his strategy to the more Loyalist south, Clinton oversaw the occupation of Charleston, South Carolina, in early May before handing command of the entire southern campaign to his famously competent subordinate Lord Cornwallis.

Clinton's plan was to consolidate Loyalist power through occupation and recruitment. The campaign was to begin in South Carolina, move upward through North Carolina and finally into wealthy Virginia, securing control of the three major coastal colonies of the south. The first stage of the campaign enjoyed success through the summer months of 1780. By late September of that year, Cornwallis had secured control of South Carolina and had just marched into Charlotte, North Carolina.

Not to say that the campaign in South Carolina did not come without its costs. The fighting in the interior had been especially bitter, with Loyalist recruits waging a bitter war against the southern Overmountain men. These early frontiersmen and guerilla fighters were from what is now Tennessee and southwest Virginia and came "overmountain" to fight the haughty rule of Imperial Britain. Rugged individualists, they had survived the perils of the wild, starvation and Indian attack with their ingenuity, toughness and skill, and were formidable opponents in the backwoods of the South.

To the British, however, they were merely savages, backwater primitives who lived beyond the pale of civilization. Yet it was precisely the arrogance of this "civilized" attitude that had driven these individualists away from the farms and towns of established society. The Loyalists and the Overmountainers were defined by radically different belief systems, and the fighting that erupted between them was especially vicious.

Colonel Patrick Ferguson was one of the senior British officers in the thick of this fighting, and in its ferocity at least, it was a kind of warfare suited to his disposition. For though Ferguson would never admit it in a hundred years, there were sides to his character that were rather similar to the Overmountainers he despised so much. Having enlisted in the military as a commissioned officer when he was 15 years old, Ferguson was a man of remarkable ingenuity, whose acute perception of the world around him tempered the restrictive discipline of military order that had been drummed into him from such an early age. In an earlier tour of the colonies, Ferguson took in the lessons of the deadly long rifle used by backwoodsmen and developed a weapon of his own design that would be able to match the range and accuracy of the weapon favored by the colonial frontiersmen. The effectiveness of his revolutionary breech-loading rifle was demonstrated to none other than King George III in 1775, but the loading method was considered too radical, and very few were manufactured.

Yet if Ferguson was possessed of the innovation and adaptability of the American frontiersman, he also inherited all of the arrogant conceit of the British Empire. When Cornwallis was still in South Carolina in the summer of 1780, he ordered Ferguson into the hills to recruit and train Loyalist sympathizers. While Ferguson was successful in marshaling thousands of locals under the king's banner, he also succeeded brilliantly in conveying his contempt for the "barbarians" who were his enemy. His attitude didn't help the situation at all. In fact, his voluble scorn for the Overmountain men could have been one more factor that led to the stiffening of Patriot resolve west of the Blue Ridge, where Ferguson's name became a hated word on the lips of every man and boy who could shoot a rifle.

For instance, when the bitter guerrilla warfare raged in the woods of South Carolina throughout the summer of 1780, Ferguson had an ultimatum delivered to Colonel Isaac Shelby, one of the Overmountain leaders. In it he warned the "officers on the Western waters" that if they didn't "desist from their opposition to the British army, and take protection under his standard, he would march his army over the mountains, hang their leaders and lay their country waste with fire and sword." Instead of cowing the proud frontiersmen on the other side the Blue Ridge, the arrogant certainty of the threat only added fuel to the fire of rebellion and became a recruiting tool for the Patriot fighters in the region.

A few months later, Ferguson's attitude caught up with him. In late September, Cornwallis, marching north from South Carolina, had established a foothold in Charlotte, North Carolina. Meanwhile, even as the Overmountain men's numbers massed against him and his Loyalists, Ferguson never dropped his assumptions of superiority. By the time he marched into North Carolina, it was obvious that Ferguson had lost his touch with the common people. On October 1, he wrote up his infamous address to the inhabitants of North Carolina, hoping to win them over to the Crown. It read:

> Gentlemen:—Unless you wish to be eat up by an inundation of barbarians, who have begun by murdering an unarmed son before the aged father, and afterwards lopped off his arms, and who by their shocking cruelties and irregularities, give the best proof of their cowardice and want of discipline; I say, if you wish to be pinioned, robbed, and murdered, and see your wives and daughters, in four days, abused by the dregs of mankind—in short, if you wish or deserve to live, and bear the name of men, grasp your arms in a moment and run to camp.

The Back Water men have crossed the mountains; McDowell, Hampton, Shelby and Cleveland are at their head, so that you know what you have to depend upon. If you choose to be degraded forever and ever by a set of mongrels, say so at once, and let your women turn their backs upon you, and look out for real men to protect them.

The message was supposed to win its readers over, but all it did was bolster support for the coming "barbarians." Colonels Charles McDowell and Isaac Shelby saw their numbers swell to over 1400 men. On the other hand, Ferguson, who commanded a Loyalist troop of fewer than 900 and was denied a request for reinforcements, was forced to assume a defensive strategy.

When Colonel Ferguson first looked on King's Mountain, he was convinced he had found the perfect defensive position. A long spoon-shaped ridge about 600 yards long, 120 yards wide on its oval end and about 60 yards wide at its narrow end, the ridge was littered with thick stands of trees and large rocks at its edges, landscape Ferguson believed would hinder his enemies' approach.

He was wrong. After marching all night through the Carolina woods, the Overmountain men converged on King's Mountain early in the afternoon of October 7. Looking at the stiff parade-style formation of Ferguson's well-trained men ringed around the top of the ridge, they knew the layout of the field was almost perfectly suited for their attack. If the slopes of King's Mountain had been bare, the Patriots would never have been able to do it. Not one man among them had the training, discipline or flat-out foolishness to march up an open plain towards a line of enemy soldiers. They were not battlefield soldiers, but Indian fighters who had learned their martial skills stalking the trees and hills of their adopted wilderness.

Thus the same trees and boulders Ferguson believed would be impediments to any concerted attack actually worked to provide cover for the Overmountain men as they made their way up the sides of the ridge. Surrounding the entire ridge, the entire Patriot force made its way up the sides of King's Mountain. They darted from boulder to tree to boulder, staying well covered from the concentrated fire of Ferguson's line, taking shots at their fully exposed enemy whenever the opportunity presented itself.

The accurate sniping of the Overmountain men began to take its toll. One by one, Ferguson's men fell where they stood, while their own fire rained ineffectually over the well-covered men below. Ferguson quickly realized that standing and shooting was getting him nothing but dead men; he knew he had to change his tactics. It was then that he realized these Patriots would have no bayonets at the end of their long rifles, and even if some of them did, they would not be trained properly in their use.

"Bayonets!" the British colonel hollered, and each of his men thrust their rifles out in front of them with a shout. "Charge!" The Loyalists poured down the sides of King's Mountain, leading with a wall of gleaming steel. It turned out that Ferguson was right about the Patriots' lack of ability or enthusiasm for this kind of close fighting. But instead of standing their ground and getting slaughtered on the tips of Loyalist bayonets, the Overmountain men just retreated down the slope, melting away in front of

Ferguson's charge, which the colonel quickly reined in before his men went too far.

"Return to positions!" Ferguson called out when the slopes had been cleared of the enemy. "Form ranks!" With admirable precision, the Loyalists fell back to their previous positions, ringed around the top of the King's Mountain ridge and waited. Sure enough, the Overmountain men emerged again, each one repeating their tentative approach up the side of the mountain. Again, rifle fire rang out from the trees below, and again, the Loyalists standing in their well-formed ranks were shot down, one after the other. Ferguson repeated the charge, with the same limited results.

By the time the Patriots began up the mountain for the third time, morale was beginning to falter among Ferguson's men. Not only did they have to endure standing on open ground while well-covered and skilled rifle men picked them off with impunity, but shots began ringing out from the narrow southwest side of the ridge that Ferguson had left undefended, assuming the sheer slope of that side of the mountain would be too steep for the enemy to scale. Evidently, the colonel underestimated the ability of the Overmountain men again, and as the gun smoke began to thicken on the undefended southwest end of the ridge, Ferguson ordered his square of solders to collapse into a tight circle around his command tent.

When the Patriots began their approach again, this time on every side, white flags of truce began to pop up here and there along Ferguson's line. But the fiery colonel would not even allow himself to think about surrendering to an enemy he held in such low regard. Saber in hand,

Ferguson would ride up to any man who was waving white and cut the color off at the staff. Mounted on a white stallion, the colonel rode up and down his line, roaring at his men to fight on. Many of his men might have done so if they could get to their enemy. But the Overmountain men remained in the cover of the slope and picked off the wide-open Loyalists.

In a last desperate attempt to turn the tide of the battle, Ferguson gathered a squad of his best soldiers and charged down the slope towards the Overmountain line, leading the way on horseback. It was suicide. Patrick Ferguson was cut down in full view of his men, sent toppling from his horse with a chest full of musket balls, dead before he hit the ground. The fate of those soldiers who charged with him was no different. As for the now thoroughly demoralized men atop King's Mountain, they were desperate to surrender, frantically brandishing white shirts and handkerchiefs. Yet the ire raised by Ferguson's arrogance outlasted him, and it took some time before the bitter Patriots stopped firing.

For all the dark words, acrimony and bad blood that existed between the two sides, King's Mountain was all over within an hour's time. Patriot casualties were numbered at 28 killed and 64 wounded, while the casualties on Ferguson's side were 157 killed, 163 wounded and nearly 700 taken prisoner. The battle was a complete defeat for the British. Not only had they lost a sizeable militia force that was a valuable supplement to Cornwallis' army farther east, but it was also the first major loss in the string of victories the Loyalists had enjoyed in the south. The annihilation of Ferguson's homegrown army cut out the legs of British influence in the Carolinas' backcountry and ultimately led to Cornwallis' withdrawal into South Carolina. Some historians have gone so far as to say that the Patriot victory at King's Mountain was the deciding factor in ensuring that the southern colonies would join the northern colonies' march to nationhood.

As for Colonel Ferguson, the Patriots forgot none of his rhetoric after the battle was over and were determined to humiliate the man who had been so eager to humiliate them. The Patriots stripped Ferguson of his uniform and took turns urinating on his dead body before burying him in a shallow ravine atop King's Mountain, piling stones atop the mound to prevent wild scavengers from getting at the body.

It turned out that it wasn't the body posterity would have to worry about. The years following the War of Independence brought no shortage of hostility between the United States and the British Empire. There was the French Revolution, the War of 1812, British sympathies with the Confederacy and more than one border dispute that broke out between the United States and Canada to the north. Nevertheless, the animosity between the two governments eventually cooled. It would take a while, but the United States and the Great Britain would become allies on the global stage.

As the War of Independence withdrew into the national memory, so too did the bile and acrimony that sustained the conflict fade. It is difficult to say for sure, but the bitterness toward Britain among the general population probably dissipated faster than it did among the ruling elite. During the years after the war, the Scots that lived around

King's Mountain took to adding more stones upon Patrick Ferguson's grave. As despicable as his sentiments might have been, many local Scots thought, he was still Scot—a proud and fiery and tough one at that—and as such, the very least he deserved was a proper Scottish burial cairn.

The reconciliation did not stop there. In 1930, on the 150th anniversary of the battle, the United States government sponsored a monument to be erected in Patrick Ferguson's honor. It stands today atop King's Mountain, a succinct national nod to the colonel's bravery on the battlefield. The monument's praise is terse. It reads "A soldier of military distinction and honor." Given Ferguson's supreme arrogance off the battlefield, however, perhaps it is a good thing that it doesn't say more. Then again, history books and monuments can only say so much. And in this case, the spirit of Patrick Ferguson seems only too glad to pick up the tale where the formal history leaves it.

He hasn't been spotted often. Today, King's Mountain National Military Park is a peaceful place—a pleasant wooded hill that rises out of the lush Carolina countryside. But the experiences of a few people at the battlefield have lent the pleasant park darker, more mysterious shades. Those who have seen him have always seen him at dusk, usually in their peripheral vision—a flash of color through the trees, moving at a brisk pace towards the cairn piled atop the mountain. The moment he appears, witnesses are seized by strange physical reactions—ranging from an inexplicable lump in the throat to chills up the back of the neck to sudden fits of nausea. But when they turn to catch a glimpse of who is there, they find themselves staring into the empty and darkening woods.

There would be no reason to believe that this elusive movement is Colonel Patrick Ferguson, but other, more dramatic sightings suggest that he calls King's Mountain home. For a few hours each day, when the darkening gray of dusk settles over the park, deepening the shadows, he has appeared right in front of people who happen to be standing around his burial cairn. He stands dressed in his full battle uniform looking exactly as he does in his portraits, a lively, somehow disturbing spark in his eye, a trace of a mischievous smile playing across his face.

In the few times he has appeared near his cairn, he has remained visible for such a short time that most eyewitnesses thought their eyes were playing tricks on them in the darkness and that maybe they didn't really see him. One second, two, and then he is engulfed by shadow, stepping back into the trees and vanishing from sight. Yet there have been a few people who, more willing to rely on their gut feelings, swear that they were staring at the famed Revolutionary War officer.

Perhaps Ferguson's elusiveness is the reason King's Mountain doesn't figure more prominently among paranormal enthusiasts. For if the ghost of Patrick Ferguson does indeed reside on the mountaintop, he is not too keen on fraternizing with those on this side of the grave.

However, according to B. Keith Toney, the author of *Battlefield Ghosts,* the ghost of Ferguson not only appeared to two Revolutionary War enthusiasts who were walking the battlefield at nightfall, he actually *spoke* to them. The two were standing in front of the cairn talking when Ferguson came out of the shadows and stopped, standing no more than 8 feet away. A few tense seconds passed before he spoke in a thick Scottish brogue, telling them that cairns don't always work in keeping the spirits of the dead from wandering. With this, he threw his head back and let out a robust laugh, then took a few steps back and vanished into the shadows of the trees.

It seems, then, that Ferguson's ghost might be a merry one—or, at the very least, one with a dark sense of humor. It is intriguing that Ferguson's ghost might laugh, given the anger and desperation he must have felt in his last earthly moments while leading his suicidal charge against an enemy that, despite all his contempt and low regard, was still about to defeat him. The fact that Ferguson's spirit was able to share a joke with his two startled witnesses suggests that, like the nation that once reviled him, Ferguson has put his loathing for his enemy behind him.

So why would his ghost still haunt the mountain where he was killed?

Is he basking in the glory of his very own monument? Is he so enraptured by the thrill of battle that he can't bear to leave the place where he last experienced it? Or perhaps he gets a kick out of scaring the daylights out of people he still believes to be the enemy? Like so many other cases of supernatural phenomena, the best we can do is ask questions and shrug. Perhaps the next person who sees Patrick Ferguson on King's Mountain will have the presence of mind to ask him why in the few short seconds he appears. Whether or not the old Scot answers, vanishes back into the trees or just tilts his head back and breaks into a laughing fit is another question all together.

The Ghostly Soldiers
of Camp Hill

By all rights, it should have been the last place in the world to put a military barracks. Located where the Potomac River meets the Shenandoah, Camp Hill was established early in the United States' history, when the territories west of the Ohio Valley were undiscovered country and generals wore powdered wigs with ponytails. It was late in the 18th century, and the lush Shenandoah Valley was just as feted for its natural beauty then as it is today. Thomas Jefferson himself called the region one of the most splendid places on earth, bragging to friends in Europe that the Virginian valley alone was worth a trip across the Atlantic.

So if the region was so valued for its verdure, why did the silk-hosed and gold-buckled elite deign to establish, of all things, a military barracks there? The decision had everything to do with the French and the proximity of Harpers Ferry. Founded by a Quaker architect by the name of Robert Harper in the mid-1700s, Harpers Ferry was one of the region's earliest settlements. By the time the United States had won its independence, it was a thriving commercial center—thriving for 18th-century Virginia, anyway. George Washington decided to give it a little kick start when he ruled that the country's first national armory would be built there. A few years later, when things started to get tense between the French and Americans, the United States government thought it might be time to beef up their military. General Charles C. Pinckney was put in charge of a portion of this new army and sent out with these troops to the national armory in Harpers Ferry. Pinckney had his men bivouacked on a ridge overlooking the town—thereafter known as Camp Hill.

Luckily, the problems with the French simmered down before things got out of hand, and the soldiers at Camp Hill were never actually called upon to turn their bayonets against the French. Whether they were relieved or disappointed at the fact, we will never know, but what is certain is that in the time they were in Camp Hill, training how to kill Frenchmen, many of them became attached to the beauty of the Shenandoah Valley. Some of them ended up building their homes in the region after their terms in the military had expired, raising families on the same ground on which they had been taught to march in time to fife and drum, fix bayonets and charge on command. How each man who stayed behind reconciled the beauty of the valley with the brutality of his training was up to him. At least all they did there was train, and the hills and waters around Harpers Ferry remained untainted by the fires of war.

Those who have studied the Civil War might know that this did not remain so. The town of Harpers Ferry served as a flashpoint between North and South when John Brown attempted to initiate a slave insurrection with his famous raid on the Harpers Ferry armory. But more than this, the hills surrounding the West Virginian town were turned into battlegrounds more than once during the course of the war. The chickens of Camp Hill

Many Civil War battles were fought in the picturesque Shenandoah Valley.

had come to roost, as the former training ground had become a full-fledged battlefield.

Union and Confederate men gave their lives on Camp Hill in the fighting, and both sides occupied the ridge at different times during the war. It turned out that Camp Hill's previous incarnation as a military encampment was only a precursor to the real thing, and soldiers swarmed into the valley when the Civil War turned its attention to the idyllic little region. It has been written that some of the military encampments were so large their nightly fires spread out in every direction as far as

George Washington had the first national armory built in Harpers Ferry, which later became the site of Civil War battles.

the eye could see—a still and eerie mirror to the starry sky above.

When the Civil War ended, life in the valley went back to normal—or as normal as could be expected. The

United States had wounds to heal, and the Shenandoah Valley was no exception, as the people of the region struggled to come to grips with the war's bloody bestowal. It was more than a matter of burying the bodies and making amends with the enemy. The war opened a deep gash in the nation, and if it had stopped bleeding, there was still the terrible scar that ran all the way down the Mason-Dixon line. The people of Harpers Ferry knew it. They knew it by the bitter divide that still existed between Northern and Southern sympathizers in West Virginia, by the Congressional debates regarding Reconstruction and by the ghosts in their backyard.

Camp Hill was never the same after the Civil War. Locals spoke of a menace in the shadows of the woods that was never there before. Solitary travelers who happened to be on Camp Hill would jump at the harsh and urgent whispers coming from the trees. Others swore they heard the sounds of some grand military procession making its way to Harpers Ferry, complete with flutes, drums and the measured tramp of soldiers' boots. Yet there were no soldiers to be seen. Even as the pounding noise of troops on the move was loud enough that hundreds, if not thousands, of men ought to have been marching right by, startled observers found themselves standing alone in the middle of a deserted road.

These occurrences seemed to get more and more common throughout the rest of the 1800s. The numerous accounts include the popular one about the late-night cavorters in Harpers Ferry. According to this tale, a number of young men from the nearby town of Bolivar were making a thorough tour of the bars in Harpers Ferry.

They kept at it until the last bar in Harpers Ferry locked its doors for the night, only then deciding to make the trek back to Bolivar. A full moon was shining that night, and the gang of drunken men navigated the road by silver light.

Camp Hill's ridge rises between Harpers Ferry and Bolivar, and the men had to cross the ridge to the other side to get home. Knowing all the stories that were circulating about Camp Hill, the men were quick to make light of their situation. As they walked they called the ghosts out of the trees, breaking out in fits of besotted laughter between renditions of Civil War songs such as "Dixie's Land." Obviously skeptical men to begin with, the drink added volume to their inclinations. They hooted and howled at the moon, laughed at the darkness, and when they were convinced no phantom soldiers would march by, played at being the soldiers themselves. They were having a ball—until the distant rap of military drums sounded over their tomfoolery.

All at one, the drums cut their revelry short, and they were all sober as Sunday morning. One of them voiced the obvious question: "What is that?" But no one answered. They all stood silent, unable or unwilling to believe their own ears as the sound got closer and closer.

"Who the hell out there's foolin' on us?" one of the men called into the darkness ahead, his voice tinged with fear. The response that came from down the road sent a jolt of panic into the boys. It came suddenly and out of nowhere, so loud that they could feel it in the ground: the sound of marching boots, thousands of them, marching in time with the drums.

"It's true!" one of the drunkards blubbered, not bothering to conceal the terror in his voice. "The stories are true! It's a damned army, a damned phantom army!"

When the fifes kicked in to accompany the drums, the young men on Camp Hill broke, turning tail and running back to Harpers Ferry. They ran fast and reckless, yet somehow it seemed as if the marching footsteps were gaining. Even though the military footfalls fell at the same relentless cadence, they got louder and louder as the men ran. The faster the men ran, the closer the phantom army got, until it seemed as if the ghosts were right on top of the terrified men.

That was when one of them tripped, stumbling over a root in the road and falling hard. He did not dare to look back, so close did the coming army seem, but rolled off the road and behind some trees. A moment later the ghostly soldiers were marching right by. Not only could he hear the drums, the fifes and the boots, he could hear their equipment as well—the metallic ring of pots and pans on backpacks, of sabers rattling in their scabbards. But not a single voice, not a whisper or a breath, or anything else that might suggest the army marching a mere 3 yards from where he lay was, in fact, real. The young man gathered his courage, took a deep breath and poked his head around the tree to take a look.

The sight froze his heart somewhere between horror and awe. There, marching right by him, was the phantom army of Camp Hill. According to the young man's frightened account, which he would eventually deliver to anyone and everyone he met, there must have been thousands of them. The men were the color of moonlight:

their uniforms, their skin, their eyes and their equipment were all different shades of luminescent silver. They all marched towards Harpers Ferry with the same blank look—stoic or dead or completely indifferent. The line of men appeared out of the darkness some 40 yards down the trail and vanished over the ridge ahead, so he was never able to see the entire line, but the soldiers just kept coming and coming, and he was stunned at the number of them. Surely his friends at Harpers Ferry could see and hear this phantom army? Certainly the front of the column should have reached town.

In fact, his friends made it into Harpers Ferry just in time, certain that the marching soldiers were right behind them. Yet when they spun around to take a look at what they were running from, they saw nothing there. In disbelief they blinked once, twice, and then the night slipped back into silence. The only one who caught site of the ghostly legion was the man who stayed up on Camp Hill. And so it is said that these soldiers are somehow bound to it, for reasons we will never know.

This supernatural encounter was only one of many to have been reported on Camp Hill. Not one year after the men from Bolivar were chased away, another pair of locals had an encounter that would earn a place in the legend of the haunted ridge. Like the men before them, these two were traveling over Camp Hill on a moonlit night, returning home to Harpers Ferry after running an errand out of town. They were approaching the crest of the ridge when they heard the sound of galloping horses coming up the other side of the hill. If there was a moment when the men refused to believe their ears, it was a moment that did not last. The ground began to shake under their feet as the thunderous sound of what must have been thousands of approaching horsemen grew louder. Their common sense told them that no such cavalry force could possibly be coming out of Harpers Ferry, but they were not about to bet this certainty against the roar of horses' hooves, the shaking trees and the trembling ground.

The two men didn't bother trying to yell their questions at each other over the roaring hooves. Realizing that survival depended on immediate action, they leapt off the trail and clambered up two trees to avoid being trampled. No sooner had they found their perches when the cavalry charged out of the darkness. They appeared suddenly and far too close, as if they had just galloped through a hole that had opened in the night less than 50 yards away. The two awestruck men could only sit, mouths agape, at the unreal spectacle before them.

It seemed as if there were thousands of them—pale riders glowing faintly of a lunar blue and silver, the sound of their horses' galloping hooves causing all of Camp Hill to shake and tremble. They moved as one thunderous body, pushing their horses forward with merciless urgency, as if the fate of all the world depended on them getting to their destination on time. And yet what was their destination? Just as they looked to be coming from nowhere, so too did they seem to vanish into nothingness a mere 30 yards from where the two men were perched. By all rights, the glowing column should have remained visible for a much greater distance, but they all seemed to be riding headlong into some black oblivion just past the crest of Camp Hill.

A large phantom army from the Civil War is still seen and heard marching near Harpers Ferry.

They rode for no cause, question or purpose. Their dead eyes were cold and devoid of any expression.

It isn't known how long the two men remained there, clutching their tree branches as the cavalry column stormed past them. What is known is that the moment they made it back home, another chapter was added to the ongoing story of Camp Hill. This wasn't the end of it, either. All around Harpers Ferry, people talked of the growing darkness on the hilltop. Every month brought more and more strange tales, and a general sense began to emerge that things were getting worse. Where the phantom soldiers had previously appeared only on the full moon, they began to be sighted on any given evening, chasing terrified witnesses off the road whether the moon was full or not.

Reports of their appearances got closer and closer to town, and there were many who believed the soldiers were coming down the hill. The ghosts themselves began to vary their activities. Some of the less-disciplined phantoms, apparently tired of being locked into their eternal march, took to haunting the surrounding houses. Terrified families living on the hill abandoned homes they were convinced had become possessed by some of these errant soldiers. These ghosts seemed to derive great pleasure from blowing their bugles into the ears of sleeping residents, discharging their weapons around the supper table and engaging each other in saber duels in kitchens and sitting rooms. While none of the residents could actually see the phantom soldiers as they invaded their homes, the clash of steel, smell of gunpowder and blast of trumpets were all real enough. The homes on Camp Hill were made uninhabitable by the ghosts that terrorized them, and each in turn was abandoned as the 19th century wore on.

Months turned to years, which turned to decades, and by the time the 20th century came to its end, the ghosts of Camp Hill had long fallen silent. Today, the strange events that are said to have taken place there are little more than well-kept legends. As dramatic as their appearances on the ridge were, the ghosts have left nothing but questions. It isn't known whether the ghosts who made their patrols over Camp Hill were Union or Confederate, defeated or victorious, damned or saved. Why did they choose the top of Camp Hill, of all places? And why did they stop?

We might never know, and in the end, it might just boil down to another legendary mystery on the much-storied Appalachian Range.

The Legend of the Headless Frenchman

Readers familiar with the legend of the Headless Frenchman might wonder why it has been included in a book about haunted battlefields. The legend finds its roots in the undiscovered country of 17th-century North America, among the flowing rivers and lush forests of what is now known as the state of Pennsylvania. Those who know their history will know that in the 1600s, no armies of uniformed men lined up in rows and columns to kill each other in the woods of Pennsylvania. The Headless Frenchman didn't meet his end at the wrong end of an Englishman's saber. No monumental clash of armies features in this story, no grand wartime tragedy that claimed lives by the thousands.

In fact, before the Headless Frenchman was in fact headless, he wasn't even a soldier, but a young adventurer following a French explorer named Étienne Brûlé into uncharted territory, hoping to make his fortune in a silver mine Brûlé's party had just discovered. But there was more than a little danger involved. For in that time, it was hazardous for Frenchmen to be traipsing around in the Pennsylvanian woods. There were Indians everywhere, and not all of them were friendly.

Étienne Brûlé knew this firsthand. He had come to America in 1614 with the famous Samuel de Champlain. Brûlé was just 16 years old, but quickly distinguished himself as the most competent frontiersman in Champlain's

French navigator Samuel de Champlain explored eastern North America, developing an allegiance with the Huron.

entourage. Over the next several years, he underwent a dangerous apprenticeship in the wild territories around the Great Lakes, acting as a scout for Champlain during the French explorer's forays into the North American interior, acting as a messenger to the many Indian tribes in the region and doing a fair bit of exploring himself. He surveyed the full length of the broad Susquehanna and went down in history as the first white man to see the Genesee River.

Besides the elements, the greatest challenge to Brûlé's passion for exploration was the Indians. Champlain made an alliance between the French and the Huron soon after he landed in North America. Unfortunately, friendship with the Huron meant rivalry with the Huron's enemy, and the Huron's enemy was one of the mightiest Indian nations in the land—the Iroquois Confederacy.

Champlain's alliance with the Huron very nearly cost Brûlé his life in the early 1600s, during one of the young man's adventures through the Pennsylvanian woods. Brûlé was captured by a group of Iroquois warriors, who quickly recognized him as a Frenchman and a friend of the Huron. They tied him to a stake and promptly went to work, branding him with red-hot irons, yanking his beard out by its roots and pulling his fingernails out. Knowing that the Iroquois intended to torture him to death, Brûlé made a desperate gamble. According to legend, he got their attention by pointing out the medallion that hung around his neck—a holy Catholic talisman depicting the Lamb of God. A burnt and bleeding Brûlé drew himself up as high as he was able and told his captors that the talisman meant that he stood in high favor with his God, and that unless they stopped torturing him and set him free, his God would exact terrible punishment.

The Iroquois wouldn't have taken the plea seriously if not for a well-timed lightning bolt and thunderclap that sounded the moment Brûlé issued his threat. Brûlé was set free and ended up living with the Iroquois for a time. Becoming fascinated with the Iroquois way of life, Brûlé went on to establish relationships with other Indian tribes, familiarizing himself with the different customs and languages along the Great Lakes. Yet though his openness to Indian cultures won him many friends, it would ultimately prove to be his undoing.

The Huron had no trust for any man who had dealings with the Iroquois, no matter what sort of talisman he might wear around his neck. Thus the Huron held Brûlé in suspicion when he returned from his time with the Iroquois. Their deep mistrust lasted for the rest of Brûlé's days. According to some versions of the story of the French explorer's life, Brûlé did not have too many days left. One legend had a group of Huron, as mistrustful as they were hungry, murdering Étienne Brûlé and then cooking his remains into a vat.

But this is a digression. The Headless Frenchman was not as illustrious a man as Brûlé, nor was he destined to become an ingredient in the bottom of a boiling cauldron. He was, however, a one-time associate of the French explorer, joining up for one of Brûlé's forays into the endless expanse of forests of the northeast. Entrenched in local legend, though never mentioned in any formal history, this particular foray led Brûlé and his men to a silver vein embedded in a wooded hill located in present-day Potter County, Pennsylvania. The tale tells us that the men found a layer of precious ore on the side of a hill deep in the woods, and promptly went about the work of converting nature's bounty into wealth. They dug a shaft into the side of the hill and constructed a primitive smelter about a mile from the shaft, where they would melt the ore into silver. It is said that the pit Brûlé's men dug nearly 400 years ago is still there, near Hammersley Valley in Potter County, along with the remnants of the smelter they had set up.

People who have gone up to take a look at what might be one of the earliest mining operations in North America are often said to remark on the determination of the miners, who would have carried the ore they dug from the shaft about a mile away to the smelter. Those people who have spent the night camping in the area during October's full moon often come down with something far more dramatic to talk about.

In the early 1600s, when Brûlé's party was pushing its way into the woods of the northeast, it might be said that much of the region was one large battlefield. The standing hostilities between Huron and Iroquois were exacerbated by the arrival of the French and English, who had their own conflicting interests. Tensions between French and English, Huron and Iroquois, continued to mount throughout the 17th and 18th centuries, until they erupted into the French and Indian War in 1754. In the time between Brûlé's explorations and the onset of open war, a multitude of unwritten and unknown atrocities occurred under the green canopies of the old northeast.

One of these atrocities was the murder of the Headless Frenchman. The details of his death are not fully known, but it must have occurred before Brûlé was taken in by the Iroquois Confederacy because the legend tells us that the perpetrators were a group of warriors from that tribe. Evidently not at all happy or impressed with the French

Étienne Brûlé discovered a silver mine in what is now Pennsylvania. One of his group is thought to haunt the area still.

party's mining operation in their territory, the Iroquois sent out a war party to shut down the enterprise. Why the Iroquois didn't wipe out Brûlé and everyone in his outfit will remain a mystery. Instead, they killed only one man.

They descended on Brûlé's camp at night, decapitating the unlucky Frenchman in his sleep. They took his body with them, leaving only his head behind. The macabre sight of the disembodied head gaping at them the next morning sent a strong message. Brûlé's men vacated the area as quickly as they could that very next morning, abandoning the mine and almost all the silver they had dug out of the side of the hill. They left in such haste that they didn't even bother to bury their comrade's head, but left it lying there, its sightless stare frozen in grisly repose.

Brûlé's dead companion might have quickly been forgotten, another nameless casualty in the early colonial struggle of the northeast. But it turned out that the tale of this Frenchman's gruesome end would survive, reaffirmed once a year, when the full moon shines in the month of October—the night the Headless Frenchman wanders the woods of Pennsylvania.

Local Iroquois were the first to see him, and they instantly knew that this was the man they had killed one year before. Shining under the silver light of fall's moon, he drifted through the settlement of those Iroquois who had taken his life. He appeared as he had in life, except that a billowing mist gathered over where his feet would be, and his head wasn't atop his neck as it should have been. The apparition carried his head in the crook of his right arm. The Headless Frenchman drifted slowly through the Iroquois settlement, leaving a trail of silver mist behind him and a fearful chill in every Iroquois he passed, before vanishing into the forest.

The Iroquois were wrong if they believed the Headless Frenchman would find peace after his first moonlit appearance. For in the following year, during the night of October's full moon, he appeared again, holding his head at his waist, drifting through the trees of the Hammersley Valley. And according to many, he has continued to appear, once a year, every year, when a full October moon shines over the Pennsylvania night.

Today, the place where he is said to appear is at the Twin Sisters, in the woods of Potter County. The Twin Sisters are two big white pines that form a natural landmark. For years, there has been a tradition among local campers and hunters to keep their distance from the Twin Sisters at night. Paranormal enthusiasts and curiosity seekers, on the other hand, have done their part to keep the legend alive. There are those who still talk about the shaft dug into a hilltop near Hammersley, the fragments of ore that can still be around this shaft and a small crumbling circle of stones about a mile away that might be the remnants of Brûlé's smelter.

And what of the Headless Frenchman himself? Does he still make his yearly walk through the woods? That depends on whom one listens to, on whom one chooses to believe. Anyone hoping to catch sight of the Headless Frenchman would have to camp out at the Twin Sisters overnight, so those who have made the trip in hopes of determining whether he actually exists tend to be the most ardently curious ghost hunters. Some of these people claim to have seen the Headless Frenchman with their own eyes, while others will swear that the only thing they witnessed when the midnight hour rolled around were a whole lot of trees. Whom do we believe? Perhaps the only way to know for sure is to wait for October's full moon, pack up a tent and sleeping bag and make the trip up to the Twin Sisters.

Death on the Mountain

This story is also found in Ghost Stories of the Civil War, *which I co-wrote with Edrick Thay (Ghost House Books, 2003) –DA*

The dread in the air was palpable on South Mountain early in the morning of September 14, 1862. Old Daniel Wise saw it in the eyes of the thousand-some North Carolinian Confederates who were frantically going to work all over his farm. They set up firing lines, dug in behind the stone wall that marked the borders of his land and carefully placed their cannons to cover the Old Sharpsburg Road where it approached the Fox's Gap mountain pass. Within an hour, Daniel's once-tranquil farm was unfamiliar to the old man's eyes. Rows of cabbage and corn vanished without a trace, trampled under the Confederate brigade and replaced by artillery batteries and walls of rifles bristling with bayonets. Every rifle was cocked and loaded, pointing southeast across Fox's Gap, towards the approaching enemy.

Not one of the soldiers said a word to Daniel Wise while they transformed his farm into a military fortress, and Wise knew better than to get in their way. Only after every fighting man was in his proper place did the commanding Confederate officer approach the overwhelmed farmer. The officer, a young man with perfectly kept dark hair and a goatee that hung past his collar, wore a gray military coat studded with two rows of brass buttons. Gold brocade wound up his sleeves and shone in the morning sun. "Good morning to you, sir," the officer said, speaking in an ebullient Virginian accent. "I am General Samuel Garland, an officer of the Confederate States of America. My brigade had been ordered to defend this pass through the mountain against the approaching enemy, and will do so at any hazard. Let me assure you that you will be reimbursed for any damage to your farm."

"Any damage to my farm," Wise mumbled as he surveyed the trampled mess that used to be his harvest.

"In the meantime," Garland continued, "I suggest you and your family leave this area as quickly as possible, for there are two brigades of bluecoats coming up the Old Sharpsburg Road, and we do not intend to let them pass without a fight."

The old farmer didn't need a second warning. Gathering his daughter and son and what personal possessions he could fit into his wagon, Wise left his small wooden cabin behind him. He could hear the opening shots of the battle as the first Union soldiers cresting the ridge of South Mountain found themselves facing General Garland's brigade.

The fight for Fox's Gap began at about nine o'clock in the morning. It was one desperate engagement in the larger battle of South Mountain, where General Lee's Confederate rearguard engaged the vastly larger Union forces under General McClellan. History would remember the fight only as a lead-in to the horrific battle of Antietam, occurring three days later just beyond the South Mountain range, but for thousands of Union and Confederate soldiers, the fight for passage through the South Mountain gaps was the end of the road. Bullets and cannonballs flew back and forth, decimating Union and Confederate lines. The relentless Union advance on General Garland's position led to fierce hand-to-hand fighting along Daniel Wise's old stone wall. Men lunged at each other with bayonets, knives and fists. General Garland himself was shot off his horse, breathing his last as his demoralized brigade finally broke out into a headlong retreat from the larger Union force.

The battle for Fox's Gap was a short affair, lasting only about two hours, but it was no less bloody for its brevity. By the time the Federals occupied the pass, hundreds of dead bodies lay thick over Wise's fields. The mountain pass was turned into a landscape of death, with soldiers shot, stabbed or blown to pieces by artillery. Union soldiers were the ones standing wearily over the battlefield after the smoke had cleared, but an onerous duty came along with victory. For though the field was theirs, so too were the fallen that covered it, and the task of burying the dead fell on their shoulders. It was hard, ugly work, made worse by the fact that the rocky ground at Fox's Gap made the digging especially difficult. Eventually, the Union men, demoralized, disgusted and exhausted by their nightmarish detail, decided they had enough. Eager to finish their burial detail, they gathered the last 58 Confederate bodies and threw them into Daniel Wise's well. After they were done their grisly work, the Union soldiers finally moved on. A few days later, on September 18, Daniel Wise and his two children returned home.

The Wise family couldn't have dreamed up a more horrific sight. The fertile fields they once knew were now unrecognizable, made into a surreal harvest of devastation by the numberless Union burial mounds in Wise's fields. Dead Confederates were buried in shallow trenches that were dug right up against the bullet-ridden walls of the Wise farmhouse. Death hung over the entire area, and there was no escaping the stench of rot that was just as thick outside Daniel Wise's cabin as it was within. But the worst of it lay at the bottom of the Wise well, where 58 dead southerners lay decomposing in the festering darkness of the dank pit.

The Civil War continued on its bloody course, leaving Daniel Wise and his ruined farm to be forgotten in the backwaters of Maryland's local history. Yet Daniel's tale did not end there. In fact, it had just begun. As outraged as he was at the mess the Union army left behind, Wise quickly learned that some of the dead on his farm were as unhappy with their burial arrangements as he was.

According to popular account, Daniel Wise's first run-in with one of the Fox's Gap ghosts occurred a few days after he arrived. Wise was sitting on the porch of his home, smoking a pipe and trying to figure out what he was going to do about his farm, when a solitary young man appeared in the distance, walking down the Old Sharpsburg Road towards his home. As Wise watched the man approach, he felt a dull chill creep up his back. He wasn't sure why, but the sight of this man filled him with a strange sense of dread. Only when the stranger drew closer did Wise begin to get an idea of what sort of thing he was facing. At about 20 yards, Wise couldn't help noticing the bone white pallor of the man's skin; a few yards closer, and Wise could make out the eerily blank expression on his face. When the pale man stepped onto

Wise's front yard, the Maryland farmer realized that he could see right through his visitor; the man before him was transparent.

Daniel Wise nearly fell out of his rocking chair in fright. "Wh-wh-who are you?" he stammered, not sure whether he should have asked *what* instead of *who*.

The visitor did not respond for long moments, and a terrifying silence settled over Wise's yard. When the transparent apparition finally did speak, its voice sounded cold and empty, like the frigid fall wind blowing over South Mountain. "Our lives were stripped from us and we were not even given a proper burial. Be sure that I will return here every night until we are honored as fallen soldiers." The apparition then slowly turned until it was looking at Daniel Wise's well, standing for a minute or two as it grew evermore transparent, until there was nothing there at all.

Frantic and terrified, Wise ran towards the well, somehow hoping to speak with the dead young Confederate, perhaps to tell him that he wasn't the one who had thrown the men in the well, that he was just as upset about how the dead soldiers had been disposed. The blood red sun was just about to dip under South Mountain when he reached the well, and the old man frantically threw the cover back.

Leaning forward into the black pit, Daniel was just about to holler his plea when the smell of putrefaction hit him. All he managed to get out was a tortured gag before he crumbled to his knees, his body unable to take in the poisonous stench of rot. He heard them then, as he was hunched against the well wall coughing and spitting. Their moans rose out of the depths of the well, a tortured chorus of hopelessness and misery. The sound was so horrific that Daniel was never able to forget it for as long as he lived.

But at that moment, all he could think of doing was closing up the well and getting as far away from it as he could. Struggling to his feet, Daniel Wise pushed the lid back over the well opening and staggered back to his cabin as fast as his shaky legs could take him. Once inside, he slammed the door shut behind him, barring the entrance with a chair jammed under the doorknob. He didn't sleep a wink that night, his thoughts plagued by the appearance of the dead Confederate and the voices in the well.

Daniel Wise never went near the well again, but the dead soldier's apparition appeared on the Old Sharpsburg Road every night, just as the sun was setting. If Daniel was outside, finishing up his daily chores or relaxing with a pipe on his front porch, the ghost turned off onto his yard and made his way towards Wise. There the dead soldier stood for several minutes, staring blankly at the Maryland farmer before gradually fading into nothingness. On those nights when Daniel was indoors at sunset, the ghost went only as far as the gates, stopping there to stare at the Wise home with the same expressionless gaze until fading out of sight.

For his part, Daniel Wise never got used to the ghost's regular appearances. Every day, he felt anxiety creeping in as the sun dipped close to the South Mountain ridge and the sky began to grow dark. Sometimes he tried to ignore the apparition, moving indoors at the first sign of dusk and drawing his shutters tight. But Wise quickly learned these measures were pointless, for even when he couldn't see the dead Confederate, he could still *sense* him—standing silently just outside his fence, looking at the shuttered window of his home with blank accusation. Wise *knew* he was out there. Gaping in fearful silence at the walls of his home, imagining the ghost standing alone on his doorstep, the old farmer found no respite locked indoors. Somehow, imagining the presence of the lone phantom was just as frightening as standing in front of it.

The Southern casualties at South Mountain turned life on the Wise farm bad. Cursed by the daily visits of the dead soldier, Daniel did everything he could to get the Confederates in the well a proper burial. He wrote letters to Washington, complaining bitterly about the mess the Union army left behind all over his land and the well that was choked with corpses. Days turned into months, which turned into years, and though Daniel Wise kept up a constant stream of correspondence, he did not hear anything back from the federal government.

Never once did he mention the ghost in any of his missives, but word of the supernatural soldier on the Old Sharpsburg Road spread through the county. More than one curiosity seeker staking out the road at sunset claimed to see him as he drifted towards Daniel's farm. Even after 1865, when North and South settled into their uneasy peace, locals still claimed to see the ghost of the anonymous soldier making his way down Fox's Gap towards Daniel Wise's farm.

The ghost continued its vigil throughout the 1860s, just as Wise continued his correspondence with Washington, demanding that something be done about the bodies. He finally received an answer in 1874. Twelve years after the last shot was fired at Fox's Gap, the United States military sent in an army detail to clean up Wise's farm; they removed the bodies from his well and exhumed the men buried on his land for proper interment.

Daniel never saw the soldier again, and for the rest of his years he enjoyed his sunsets in peace, content in knowing that his efforts granted the Confederate dead their final rest. His story, however, lived on. After Daniel Wise passed away, the tale of the ghostly soldier became a local legend. Wise's house was eventually flattened, his farm abandoned and his well buried. But the burial and reburial of the Confederate casualties at Fox's Gap is still noted as one of the Civil War's more grisly footnotes, and the tale of the old farmer and his nightly visitor remains, though it has been over a century since any phantom footsteps made their way down the Old Sharpsburg Road.

The Phantom Horseman at the Brandywine

No one knows for certain who the horseman is, when he made his first appearance or why he lingers on the Brandywine battlefield. But he has been appearing for years, for as long as anyone can remember, always on horseback, always on nights when a full moon shines, always in the Pennsylvania fall. Some have seen him crossing Chadds Ford, bedecked in anachronistic military dress—tricorne, white knee pants, blue long coat with rows of brass buttons, a saber bouncing against his horse's flank. His solitary crossing of the Brandywine River is a strange and eerie thing to behold. Commanding a stiff and jaunty canter over Chadds Ford, the horseman sits unnaturally straight, barely moving along with the mechanical, somehow unnatural rhythm of his bright white horse. Both man and beast stare straight ahead, impassive, unseeing, pale as the moon, and though the Brandywine's waters splash around the horse's legs, neither horse nor rider makes a sound.

He has also been seen in the Brandywine Valley on the east side of the river. There, startled witnesses have spotted him galloping through the woods at breakneck speed, weaving in and out of trees, leaping over broad depressions. It is always the incredible speed of the horseman that strikes onlookers here. Rider and horse are said to move so fast that they leave a blur of silvery white light behind. And even as the rider tears through the fall forest,

Under a full moon, the silvery white specters of a horse and rider are seen crossing the Brandywine River.

his face is pale and emotionless, his horse makes no sound with its passing. He is always seen heading north along the Brandywine River, moving with unearthly urgency for some unknown purpose.

And then there are the sightings along U.S. Route 1, where the highway intersects with the Brandywine battlefield. There motorists driving at night have spotted the galloping horseman in their headlights, heading northeast for Philadelphia. The rider is in the middle of the road, crouched low over his white steed, the coattails of his Continental Army uniform streaking behind him. Startled drivers invariably swerve away from the rider as they pass, staring in wonder at the glowing horseman, who looks ahead, seemingly oblivious to the passing vehicle. Yet when transfixed motorists hoping to catch a final look at the 18th-century soldier look into their rearview mirrors, they invariably see nothing but a dark, empty highway—the sudden disappearance of the horseman hitting them like a sharp slap.

The fact that this phantom rider has appeared on Route 1 has led some paranormal enthusiasts to suggest that Brandywine's horseman might be none other than the ghost of General Mad Anthony Wayne. Indeed it is true that Pennsylvania's most storied soldier figures prominently in a supernatural legend that has the famous general galloping from the southeast corner of the state to the town of Erie in the northwest. As legend has it, old Mad Anthony has been spotted by countless motorists over the years, galloping along Route 322, looking for the bones that were lost when his dead body was transported from Erie to his hometown of Radnor. If General Wayne makes yearly forays along Route 322, why not Route 1 as well, along the battlefield where he suffered one of the greatest defeats of his career?

British General William Howe declined to cross the Brandywine River at Chadds Ford for fear of encountering Mad Anthony Wayne.

That defeat came through no real fault of his own. He had received his orders from none other than Commander-in-Chief of the Continental Army, George

Washington, who told him to hold Chadds Ford against the approaching British army, under the British Commander-in-Chief, Lieutenant General Sir William Howe. The British were marching on Philadelphia, and Washington's army was the only thing that stood between Howe and the largest city of the 13 colonies. Washington intended to make his stand at the Brandywine River and appointed his favorite general, Mad Anthony, at Chadds Ford, where he was certain the redcoats would attempt to cross.

If General Anthony Wayne had not been there, Howe probably would have forded the Brandywine at Chadds, but he decided against it when his scouts reported that the fierce warmonger was entrenched on the other side of the ford with an entire division of Pennsylvania Continentals. The scouts also informed Howe that all the fords along the Brandywine were guarded by Washington's men, except, that is, for a crossing called Jeffries' Ford, located a mere 8 miles north of Washington's position. Failing to guard Jeffries' Ford was a colossal oversight on Washington's part, and one that might have been easily avoided; all the American general need have done was consult one of the locals under his command, any one of whom would have informed him of all the paths across the Brandywine. But as it was, Washington's ignorance of Jeffries' Ford left his right flank wide open for attack.

Howe was quick to pick up on Washington's error and moved promptly to exploit the glaring weakness in the Continentals' defense. Splitting his army into two divisions, Howe placed Baron Wilhelm Knyphausen in command of one 6800-man division, while a larger 8000-man

Some paranormal enthusiasts believe the phantom horseman crossing the Brandywine River is none other than Mad Anthony Wayne.

division was put under command of General Charles Cornwallis. Howe ordered Knyphausen to continue east on the road they were on and engage General Wayne at Chadds Ford, just as Washington had planned. In the meantime, while the Continentals were dealing with Knyphausen, Howe would accompany Cornwallis and his 8000 men north along the Brandywine past Washington's right flank to Jeffries' Ford, where they would cross undetected and attack Washington's exposed right side.

It was a classic flank attack, which General Howe managed to execute with near flawless precision. Knyphausen was successful in convincing Washington and Wayne that they were fighting the entire British force at Chadds Ford, while the bulk of Howe's army moved north, unbeknownst to Continental command. By the time the Americans grew wise to the fact that Howe had split his army in two, 8000 redcoats were looming behind them with bayonets set, ready to attack the rear of Washington's army. The Americans offered up a desperate defense, with all of the reserve hastily forming to meet the new threat, but Washington's men quickly crumbled into disarray under the combined assault of Knyphausen's soldiers from across Chadds Ford and Howe's soldiers from behind. The last hours of the battle saw General Mad Anthony Wayne in fine form. Possessed by the same battle lust that had won him his moniker, the legendary general was galloping back and forth across the field, rallying pockets of men together to continue the fight. If the battle was as good as lost for the Americans, Mad Anthony Wayne refused to acknowledge it, and any man who stumbled onto him in the dying moments of Brandywine would never forget the homicidal fire in his eyes, his roaring insistence that they continue the fight.

Yet all the fighting spirit in the world wouldn't turn the tide for the Americans on September 11, 1777. Brandywine was a complete and utter defeat for George Washington and his Continental Army. The battle along the picturesque Pennsylvanian river would go down as the largest land engagement during the War of Independence, with casualties of over 1000 American and nearly 2000 British soldiers. Burdened by the duty of advance and attack, Howe's men suffered heavier losses than the Americans. Nevertheless, the Battle of Brandywine was a tremendous strategic victory for the British, as Washington's defeat cleared the way to Philadelphia. Two weeks later, on September 26, Howe's men marched into the colonial capital and claimed it for the Crown.

Of course, Brandywine and the occupation of Philadelphia was only a temporary setback for the Americans. The colonies ended up winning their independence from the British, and George Washington was unanimously chosen as the first president of the United States. Still, Brandywine continues to survive in the annals of military history, a model of a classic flanking procedure and a lesson about the importance of knowing the terrain to be fought upon. And, of course, the engagement remains a curiosity to those who have glimpsed the mysterious horseman riding over the battlefield when a full autumn moon shines over the Brandywine.

Many paranormal enthusiasts believe that the phantom horseman is the spirit of General Mad Anthony Wayne. Possessed by his legendary fervor for battle, utterly refusing to admit defeat and being defeated nonetheless, General Wayne might have been haunted by the loss at Brandywine for the rest of his life. Might he have returned to the old battleground after he died, nearly 200 years later? Still mulling over the details of his defeat, crossing and recrossing Chadds Ford, obsessing over what he might have done differently? Or perhaps, on other nights, pushing his spectral steed to a gallop through the woods, down Route 1, reliving his manic attempt to quell his troops' rout and bring them back to fight their foe?

There are other theories regarding the identity of the rider, stemming from the fact that a good number of eye-witnesses who have spied the horseman claim that he is actually headless! More than once, terrified onlookers have stared in awestruck silence as the headless rider gallops through the woods. He wears 18th-century military dress, rides a glowing white mount and holds a shining saber aloft. The rider is never visible for more than a dozen seconds, disappearing into the trees moments after he appears. If the Brandywine rider is indeed headless, then it is doubtful that this is the apparition of Mad Anthony Wayne, who died after a gout attack in 1796, with his head still firmly attached to his neck.

Could it be that there are two different horsemen who haunt Brandywine—one, the famous Pennsylvanian general, the other some anonymous casualty who lost his head in the fighting? Or could it be that the headless rider is one and the same as the ghost that managed to keep its head? Maybe this apparition is eternally reliving the last moments of its life, appearing as he was before and after his death, his nighttime ride continuing for only a few seconds after his head is blown off. This might explain why the rider has been spotted more often with his head intact, and why he only appears for such a short time after he is decapitated.

One or two riders, headless or no—the ghostly phenomenon continues to haunt the Brandywine. It might be the ghost of the famed Mad Anthony Wayne or some anonymous soldier who was gruesomely killed on the battlefield over 200 years ago. Like so many explanations for paranormal phenomena, these are mere supposition. All the same, whatever the nature of the haunting, it has managed to keep this episode of American history alive. The phantom horseman's solitary ride over the moonlit Brandywine is an eerie reminder to all of the bloody origins of the nation.

The Flying Coffin

This enduring West Virginia legend originated over a century ago. A tale of violence and vengeance, the dark fable has survived generations to become a timeless allegory for the bloody and intensely personal fighting particular to the back woods of West Virginia during the Civil War.

The history of West Virginia's origins and its entry into the Civil War is recounted in more detail in *Ghost Stories of the Civil War* (Ghost House Books, 2003). Suffice it to say that the conflict that followed West Virginia's entry into the Civil War was harsh, chaotic and intensely personal. It was the worst guerrilla warfare—North versus South, backcountry feuding and indiscriminate thieving, all rolled up into one ugly package. West Virginia was officially on the side of the Union, but the fighting within made it obvious that anti-slavery sentiments weren't shared universally. On April 20, 1863, the situation got worse. Confederate General John D. Imboden led a raid from Virginia into the newly formed state. He rode in at the head of a force of over 3000 men, with the objective of disabling the B & O Railway and dissolving the state government in Wheeling by force. He was supported by General William E. Jones and his 1400 men who embarked for West Virginia the very next day. For nearly three weeks, the Jones-Imboden raid cut through West Virginia, leaving a trail of death and desolation in its wake.

It was in the path of this brutal invasion that the legend of the flying coffin was born. There was a single infantry captain under General Jones' command who had distinguished himself in every fight along the way. He had been among the leading columns when Jones captured Morgantown, destroyed the oil stores at Burning Springs and demolished the railroad bridge at Fairmont. He had seen the worst fighting of the raid up close, standing firm as men fought and died all around him.

Like so many other men who found a way to survive the brutal conditions of the Civil War, this officer had learned to cope with its horrors, shutting out all instances of terror and tragedy, thickening his skin against the suffering. Dedicated to winning the war for the Confederacy, he also made himself into an instrument of death and set his heart against mercy or compassion for any man who wore a blue uniform. As far as he was concerned, the Northerners were invaders threatening to destroy his people's way of life, and the Union sympathizers in West Virginia were worse than that. They were traitors.

And so this man went into West Virginia with a heart of stone, killing his enemy without pause or remorse. He was good at his work and cut down scores of Union men throughout the course of the Jones-Imboden raid. The Confederate captain didn't think much of the soldiers he killed. Whether they died by the edge of his saber or were shot to death across a stretch of embattled territory, they were a faceless enemy to the soldier who took their lives.

Except for one. He was a young fighting man in league with a band of West Virginia guerrillas. History has forgotten this man's name, while legend only tells us that he was barely 20 years old and that his older brother fought in the same unit. The two brothers were close and went to war with the unspoken vow that they would look after one another in battle. It was these brothers' unit that was lying low in the West Virginian woods, waiting on one side of a winding road as the Confederate captain's company approached.

The Union guerrillas held their fire until they could see the stubble on their enemies' faces. The opening volley of their ambush was devastating, but those Confederates that still stood rallied around their captain and charged into the woods. They met their assailants with set bayonets and sabers and revolvers. The fighting was close, and the Confederate captain was in the thick of it. He lunged into the trees with his sword in one hand, his pistol in the other, carving a path through the Union bushwhackers' ranks. The captain didn't look twice at the young man who rushed at him with a gleaming bayonet, but casually leveled his revolver and fired, shooting the youngster through the heart and killing him instantly.

Like so many others, the young man died without a sound, but the awful shriek that sounded above the din of battle the moment he hit the ground was like nothing the Confederate captain had heard before. He spun around to see an older version of the man he had just killed. It was the dead man's brother; he was about 20 yards away and bearing down fast, bolting through the carnage of fighting and dying men to where the Southern officer stood. There was murder in his eyes. The captain raised his gun and pulled the trigger, but all that came was a metallic click. His revolver was empty.

"Come on then!" he called across to the livid man who was now a mere 10 yards away, raising his saber in challenge. They would have fought then and there, but the larger battle that raged all around them interceded, and the two men were swept apart when a company of Confederate reinforcements arrived. The Confederate captain caught a glimpse of the enraged man roaring bloody murder through the musket fire and clashing steel. And then he was gone, lost in the rush of the gray coats that flooded into the woods.

The battle was over before it started, but the engagement left an indelible impression on the Confederate captain. Since the war began, he had witnessed every kind of atrocity. Indeed, he knew that he had committed a good number of atrocities himself. This was the face of war, he told himself. This was man at his worst. There was no need to dwell on the necessary brutalities. Each side would do what was needed to win. For this man, it had always been that simple. And yet there was something about what had just happened in the woods of West Virginia that troubled him deeply. It was in the Union guerrilla's scream at the death of his brother. It was the red-faced loathing of the man as he ran at the captain to claim his vengeance. The emotion of the war had penetrated his shell of stoicism: the sorrow, loss and hatred, raw and roiling and out of control. He stood there shaking in his boots, somehow certain that he wouldn't live through the fighting. At that moment, he wondered if any man would.

While the captain was having his revelation, the bereaved Union guerrilla was taking a solemn vow over the dead body of his brother. He had managed to make his way to his brother's body and, in the last hectic moments of the battle, carry his dead sibling away. Engulfed by grief and hatred, the man swore vengeance.

No matter how long it took, he would kill the man who cut down his brother.

The Jones-Imboden raid pushed on into West Virginia through the following week, but neither the Confederate captain nor the Union guerrilla was concerned with the war effort any longer. Both were locked in their own private war. The Union man was obsessed by thoughts of revenge; the Confederate knew, beyond any doubt, that there was a man somewhere in the woods who was bent on killing him and him alone. The guerrilla's vicious rancor grew daily. Day and night, he dreamed of vengeance, unable to think of anything but the face of his enemy. Meanwhile, the Confederate captain began to lose his resolve for the Southern cause. He foundered in the well of his own conscience, unable to justify the brutality of the war he was fighting. He started to believe that no cause was worth this amount of suffering. Fate would soon bring them together.

About one week later, Jones and Imboden had reached the limit of their advance into West Virginia. All Confederate units were ordered to pull back. The Union guerrilla, suddenly seized by the fear that he might never get the chance to avenge his brother, became reckless. At night, he went on one-man raids into Confederate camps, looking for the face he couldn't forget. He led more than one ambush on the Southerners as they pulled back, always keeping his eyes peeled for the man who killed his brother. Only when Jones and Imboden had withdrawn, and the Union man lost all hope for revenge, did he stumble on his quarry.

During the last days of the James-Imboden raid, the captain decided he wanted nothing more to do with the war and deserted the Confederate army. He turned himself in to a group of Union soldiers, who promptly bound him and put him in a wagon train with wounded and captured Confederate soldiers. But the repentant officer wouldn't get off so easily.

At first, the guerrilla didn't believe his eyes when he caught sight of the hated captain bouncing along in the back of a prisoner's wagon. Incredulous and stunned, he sat impassively on his horse, letting his mount carry him down the trail, past the long train of surrendered Confederates. His heart pounded heavily in his chest as each second took him farther and farther away from the object of his vengeance. Could that have been his man? He slowly stood up in his stirrups and took a look back.

It was him. His scabbard and pistol holster were empty. He was unarmed. Helpless. But he was also the same man who had taken his brother's life—the man he had sworn to kill.

Without another thought, the Union man drew his revolver and wheeled his horse around. Trotting back along the length of his retreating line, the guerrilla drew up to the wagon that held his hated opponent. The Confederate was given only a moment to register the barrel leveled at his head before the avenging soldier squeezed the trigger. The captain was killed instantly, the Union sympathizer's slug lodged in his skull.

In normal times, the guerrilla might have been arrested, but these were hardly normal times. The murder was merely another vile act in a time and place that was defined by them, and not a single man voiced a peep of protest as the bushwhacker holstered his gun and spurred his horse back to the front of the column. A profoundly changed man after the loss of his brother, this guerrilla made like the captain he had killed and decided to desert the Union cause. He laid down his arms and headed west, never to return to West Virginia for the remainder of the war.

It was only several years after the Civil War was over that the former Union guerrilla returned to the Mountain State. For reasons that we will never know, this man decided to make West Virginia his home, and he ended up settling down very close to the place where he avenged his brother. We can only guess what moved him to do it. Most of us would assume that he would want to get as far away as possible from such a bloody tragedy. Perhaps he had never gotten over the incident; perhaps his character had been so wholly reshaped by his experience in West Virginia that, unable to forget it, he was irresistibly drawn to where it all transpired. Maybe it was his way of getting as close as he could to his deceased brother. Or maybe the events of his past haunted his conscience, and he reasoned he would best be able to kill his demons if he moved back to the site of the tragedy.

His motives will forever remain a mystery, but whatever his reasons, in his worse nightmares, he would not have dreamed what awaited him. According to the legend, his first few months in West Virginia went well. He built himself a home, bought livestock and planted the seeds of a humble harvest on his small plot of land. He even met a young woman he took a liking to. She lived in a nearby village down the road. At the end of each week, he made the trip to this young woman's home, where he had dinner with her family and afterwards took long walks with her through the woods and hills that he had once fought over.

Things might have gone well for this man if not for the sins of his past and the route he took to this woman's home. Every week, his Sunday ride took him past a cemetery that contained the body of the Confederate captain that he had killed. The former guerrilla had no way of knowing who was buried there, but every time he rode by the graveyard's iron gate, a sudden chill ran up his spine and he was overcome by a sense of unease. His eyes were drawn, irresistibly, past the fence, through the bushes and trees, to the sight of the headstones mounted atop a dismal row of burial mounds. His gaze always settled on the same grave—the one in the farthest corner of the cemetery, shrouded in the semi-darkness of shade and surrounded by a thick growth of weeds and brambles. The sight of this one grave always filled him with a strange dread, where his mind would involuntarily drift back to the horrors of the Civil War. It was then that the face of the man who had killed his brother would come back with frightful clarity—unarmed and resigned to peace, staring helplessly into the muzzle of his revolver. An effort was always required to snap himself out of such ruminations. Forcing his gaze away from the unsettling grave, the ex-guerrilla spurred his horse and trotted away from the cemetery, willing himself to forget again.

It was always worse on his way back from the woman's home than it was on the way there. If the graveyard was unsettling to the man in daylight, it near terrified him at night. The fear descended the moment the iron gates came into sight. Though he couldn't see into the cemetery in the darkness, he was possessed by a horrifying certainty that some seething wickedness loomed in the darkness, just out of sight. Again, his mind was filled with images of the man he had killed, but this time his victim wasn't frightened and helpless, but livid, bent on violence and very badly decomposed.

Every Sunday night, he approached the cemetery with the same attitude, thinking positively, hoping that the intangible terror might not manifest itself on that night— but every time he was wrong. Indeed, not only did the fear seize him each time, but it seemed to get worse and worse. With each passing week, he grew more certain that there actually was someone, or something, lurking in the darkness of the graveyard. His terror mounted as the shape hovering in the darkness became clearer and clearer. Though he did his best to deny it, week by week a figure was emerging from the blackness of the cemetery— a being he couldn't comprehend, only knowing that whatever it was, it held nothing but malice for him. We might assume that such an experience would impel the man to stop making the trip, but he remained determined to court his belle, even if that meant passing the graveyard. His resolve would prove to be his undoing.

The apparition emerged from the cemetery on a Sunday evening late in the month of October. There was a chill in the air that night, and the man approached the graveyard on the way back from the woman's house with the same trepidation he always did. Even as he tried to convince himself that nothing out of the ordinary was going to happen, an undeniable dread was taking shape in his mind. By the time the wrought iron gate emerged from the darkness on the side of the road, every muscle in his body seemed to tell him to turn around. Quelling his urge to run, the Virginian spurred his horse forward, looking at the pitch black cemetery out of the corner of his eyes as his horse trotted along the trail.

His horse saw it first, and the sight caused the panicked animal to rear up on its hind legs, dump its surprised rider and gallop away as fast as it could. It was the first thing the ex-Union man saw when he looked up from where he lay, and the realization of what it was sent his mind spinning in a gyre of fear. Standing there, atop a floating coffin that hovered about 3 feet off the ground, was a rotting semblance of the Confederate captain who had killed his brother. He could tell it was him by the man's reddish brown beard and short tussled hair, by the filthy white cloth that was tied around his leg, by the gaping bullet hole between his eyes. In all other respects, what stood before him was nearly unrecognizable—a living corpse standing on rotting legs, staring down at his unhorsed killer with a look of unmitigated hatred burning within two badly decomposed eyeballs.

The man lay paralyzed in fear, so overwhelmed by his terror that he was unable to will his body into motion. And then the corpse moved, or rather the hovering coffin it was standing atop moved. It started slowly, so slowly that, initially, the man failed to realize that it was coming towards him. But when the rotting southern soldier bent down on creaking legs and reached out for him with one skeletal arm, the former guerrilla was shocked into action. He realized then that just as he had taken this Confederate soldier's life in vengeance, so did this ghoulish monster intend to take his. Scampering away from the dead soldier, the terrified man quickly got to his feet and ran away, going pell-mell down the trail.

He didn't make it far. Casting a glance over his shoulder, he could see that the corpse wasn't far behind. It was still standing on its coffin, which was moving after him fast and about to overtake him. He ran harder, but the rotting ghoul continued to gain on him, a hideous grin now stretched across its face. In the next instant, the man felt the speeding casket jam against the back of his knees, causing him to tumble back, so that he lay prone atop the coffin along with the corpse, flying through the dark forest. The last thing this poor man saw was the ghost of the Confederate soldier looming over him as it reached down and held his head within its vice-like grip. With the other, it reached into the hole in its head and pulled out the bullet that had ended its life. Slowly, deliberately, it brought the lead slug to its enemy's forehead. The former guerrilla's anguished scream echoed through the woods and the hills as the ghoul pressed the old bullet through his skull and into his brain.

A crisp fall morning dawned the next day, with the brilliant reds and oranges of the Appalachian range blazing under the clear blue sky. Nestled under the trees' auburn canopy, the cemetery with the iron gate was eerily still. Its rows of headstones stood the same as always, their burial mounds littered with leaves. All was as it should be, except for the strange stillness in the graveyard, where it seemed that neither a mole nor a mosquito stirred, and the one grave in the corner, which had obviously been disturbed the night before. The burial mound had been dug up violently, leaving a pit 6-feet deep, with dirt spread out in every direction, as if there had been an eruption from within the ground. The coffin in the bottom of the hole was marred with splinters and claw marks along its lip, its hinges crooked and loose. One might have thought that grave robbers had been at work, and indeed, the first West Virginians who discovered the scene would have assumed as much—an assumption that was instantly dispelled when the coffin was opened. For lying within was the body of the former Union fighting man, his face twisted into a look of unspeakable horror and a large bleeding hole drilled between his eyes. There was no trace of the body that had been buried there before.

The Ghost of Mongaugon

The War of 1812 suffered no shortage of martial drama. During this war, British troops invaded and occupied Washington, D.C., where they razed most of the city's government buildings and sent President James Madison running for the hills. During this war the Canadians under General Isaac Brock took over Detroit by outbluffing a timid American general named William Hull, who was mortified at the idea of fighting Tecumseh, the famous Shawnee war chief, and all the Potawatomi, Ottawa, Kickapoo, Delaware, Wyandot and Shawnee warriors allied with the British. The War of 1812 saw famed future president Andrew Jackson win his place among America's exalted military heroes when, with only 4000 men under him, he defeated Sir Edward Packenham and his army of 10,000 soldiers at the Battle of New Orleans.

Despite all the extraordinary military feats, there was very little at stake in the War of 1812, and the conflict ended up deciding almost nothing. Unlike the War of Independence or the American Civil War, no grand ideological cause fueled the War of 1812. A conflict that erupted over a long list of gradual grievances between the United States and the British Empire, the war was not a clash driven by the sort of fundamental ideological agreements that lie at the heart of almost every major war; rather, it was more like a violent settling of accounts.

No one event was responsible for the outbreak of hostilities, but a combination of factors, ranging from the lingering British presence in the United States' western territories to the disruption of America's ocean-going trade by British naval blockades over Napoleonic Europe. Anti-British sentiment had grown so much in the United States that the 1810 Congressional elections saw the appointment of a large number of representatives who advocated war as the solution. Led by prominent politicians such as John C. Calhoun from South Carolina, the Congressional War Hawks believed that the United States could force Britain to change its policy by an invasion of Canada. On June 18, 1812, President Madison signed a declaration of war passed by Congress. So began the War of 1812.

The following tale is set in this conflict. It is one of Detroit's oldest folktales, and there's no way to know who told it first, but throughout the 1800s, it was written and rewritten and written again, until 1884 when Marie Caroline Watson Hamlin penned the definitive version of the story in her book *Legends of Le Détroit*. Since then, the tale has largely fallen by the wayside, though it is still acknowledged among those who have an interest in folklore, and, of course, those who believe they've seen the ghost of Mongaugon.

It was early August 1812, and things were starting to heat up around the Detroit River. Earlier that summer the infamous American general William Hull had launched an attack across the river onto Canadian soil. Hull successfully captured the town of Sandwich uncontested, but he hesitated there. Much to the dismay of the officers under him, Hull began exhibiting near crippling apprehension once the army was on Canadian soil. The same man who had earlier proclaimed that no quarter would be given to any Canadian fighting alongside Indians was suddenly tortured by the prospect of fighting Indians himself. Reports of the ferocity of the Indian attacks on United States' supply convoys were exactly what Hull did not need to hear. In spite of his subordinates' pleas to attack the Canadian garrison at Fort Malden, Hull ordered the withdrawal. On August 7, his soldiers slunk back across the river to safety behind the walls of Fort Detroit.

While the humiliating retreat was demoralizing for the 2200 soldiers under Hull's command, it galvanized his opponent, General Isaac Brock, and the Canadians serving under him. Outnumbered by at least 1000 men, Brock and Tecumseh made for Detroit soon after the American general's retreat. There, in the days before Fort Detroit's infamous surrender to a force nearly half its size, the story of the ghost of Mongaugon was born.

The legend tells us that there was a young Canadian lieutenant known only by his last name, Muir, who had been stationed near the Detroit River for a few months. In that time, he had gotten to know a young woman named Marie McIntosh, the daughter of a respected Scottish trader. Actually, to say the pair got to know each other is a bit of a stretch, because they had to contend with not only the rules of 19th-century conduct but Lieutenant Muir's painful shyness around women as well.

For her part, Miss McIntosh was interested in the dashing young officer, and she was sure that every time he came to visit, she had made it painfully obvious. Yet the awkward lieutenant was frustratingly inept at returning her covert flirtation, and as much as the young woman was taken with him, she also began to tire of his courteous distance, of all his stiff social proprieties.

Not that Muir was trying to come across as a hopeless bore. Indeed, she was the sole reason he made his weekly visits to the McIntosh house. But as much as he wanted to spend time with Marie McIntosh, he was also scared witless by her. It was a classic case of lovesick jitters, and every time Muir found himself in the same room as Miss McIntosh, he might as well have been facing a row of American riflemen.

When war broke out with the Americans, however, Lieutenant Muir got the feeling that he might not have the luxury of time. Soon enough, his hunch proved to be right. In the first week of August, when General Hull was still vacillating between attack and retreat in Sandwich, the local military brass and Wyandot war chiefs were planning a raid on Mongaugon, a small American settlement across the Detroit River. It was decided that a contingent of British troops and Wyandot warriors would paddle across the river on the evening of August 9 and set upon the village of Mongaugon under cover of darkness. Young Lieutenant Muir was chosen to lead the British vanguard.

It was a dangerous mission, and Muir's commanding officers did not need to tell him it that he might not come back alive—the young man could see it in their eyes. So it was that the moment the briefing was over, he resolved to head straight over to the McIntosh house and tell Marie exactly how he felt about her. With the specter of imminent death hanging over his head, he somehow felt an affirmation of the heart might strengthen his spirit in the coming fight—might ease the agony of his passing, should it come.

Without a thought to the consequences, Lieutenant Muir mounted his horse and galloped to the McIntosh mansion, where he found Marie alone on the grounds.

The young woman knew something was up the moment she saw Muir striding up to her. It was then that the last several months of infatuation came pouring out, as the lieutenant fell to one knee and offered up every sentiment in his covetous heart. And yet Marie McIntosh was unaffected, or at least the artful coquette pretended to be. It is impossible to say whether his ardor so surprised her she needed a moment or two to think, she thrilled at the opportunity of playing coy or she was being playfully vengeful for all the months of Muir's distant formality, but after the lieutenant finished spilling his guts, she just laughed and turned away.

Incredulous, Muir got up and took a step forward. He was about to ask her for an explanation. Had he imagined every stolen glance and playful smile? Had he invented the chemistry between them? He wanted to ask. But his proper upbringing kicked in the moment he was about to open his mouth, and instead of asking for an explanation, he straightened himself, bid Marie farewell and walked stiffly away.

Of course, this mortified young Marie. While she was merely playing hard to get, Lieutenant Muir was playing Greek tragedy, and after it dawned on her that he wasn't coming back, she ran out to the front gate. Hoping to catch Muir in time to tell him that she was only joking, that of course she felt the same way, Marie got there just in time to see her humorless lieutenant galloping down the lane. A dark cloud passed over her at the sight of him riding away. Her thoughts then took an unusually serious turn, and she knew that she would never forgive herself if this was the last time she was to see him.

Well, it wouldn't exactly be the last time. That night, she could get no sleep. Her father had spoken at dinner about how some local Indians and soldiers were making a raid across the Detroit. The news instantly made her feel sick, and her voice shook when she asked if he knew which soldiers were making the attack. Mr. McIntosh, oblivious to his daughter's anxiety, smiled and told her he had no idea who would be participating in the attack, that the British military wouldn't let that kind of information out, even to men of his station. But the sinking feeling in Marie's stomach was the only answer she needed. Somehow, she knew that Muir was taking part in this raid, and her heart sank when she thought that his going to fight might have been the reason behind his earlier visit and declarations.

Marie didn't sleep well at all that night. Visions of Muir's face as he made his passionate pleas earlier that day kept her awake. In the midnight hour, she imagined him paddling across the Detroit River at the head of a troop of men, creeping onto American soil and leaping into action against the enemy. She prayed fervently for his safety at the same time as she cursed the frivolous tendencies. Demons of regret and worry toyed with the tossing and turning Marie McIntosh, until she slipped into a shallow, troubled sleep.

She wasn't asleep for long when the sound of someone shuffling into her room woke her. She sat up in bed and gasped in shock at the sight of a man standing near the foot of her bed. He was tall and was dressed in a military uniform, that much she could see from the moonlight in her room, but the man's face was shrouded in darkness.

"Excuse me sir…" she began, about to petition to the rules of propriety. That was when the man stepped forward, revealing himself fully in the silver light that streamed in through her window.

Marie let out a horrified gasp at the sight of the man standing there before her. It was her Lieutenant Muir as he had appeared in life: tall, dark-haired and strikingly dressed in the fine high-collared uniform of the British Empire. But at the same time, he was a complete stranger—his skin white as bone, a vacant lifelessness in his eyes and a gaping bullet wound in his forehead, which sprouted a line of thick black blood that streamed down across his face. She went mute in horror.

Then this deathly likeness of Muir spoke, and his voice, cold and hollow, chilled Marie to the bone. His words, as quoted by Hamlin in her 1884 book, arc written here: "Fear not, Marie, I fell tonight in honorable battle. I was shot through the head. My body lies in a thicket. I beg you, rescue it from the despoiling hand of the savage and from the wild beasts of the forest…Farewell, may you be happy."

As icy and abrupt as he ever was in life, the ghost of Lieutenant Muir then turned to go. Yet before he took a single step, he stopped. Turning back, he approached Marie McIntosh and did something that he had never dared to do while living. Stretching one scarlet-clad arm toward her, he reached out and pressed his hand against hers. His hand was so cold against Marie's skin that it felt as if he had burned her. Marie let out a scream of pain and then fainted.

The incident was the first thing in Marie's mind when she woke the next morning, and at first, she thought it had been a dream. And then she remembered Muir's touch and realized that her right hand was throbbing. Looking down, Marie went cold when her eyes fell on her wounded limb. Exactly where he had touched her was a scar like a brand, the imprint of his hand.

This time, Marie didn't swoon in horror but leapt into action. Recalling Muir's dying request, she threw some clothes on, called for her horse and, with a frantic servant barely keeping up, made for General Brock's camp at Fort Malden. While sure that no British soldier worth his name would willingly escort a woman of McIntosh's station into hostile territory, Marie knew that the Indian warriors at Malden would not hold the same reservations. She sought out a Wyandot war chief named Walk in the Water, a friend of her father's who had led the Indian fighters in the previous night's raid. After surprising Walk in the Water with her knowledge of Muir's demise, she persuaded the Wyandot chief to escort her across the river to the battlefield.

Impressed by the young woman's determination, Walk in the Water gathered a small group of warriors together and shuttled her across the Detroit River. With all the certainty of a soldier who had fought in the battle the night before and saw exactly where his commanding officer was cut down, Marie made her way across the contested ground to a thicket by the Detroit. There she found Lieutenant Muir lying dead with a bullet in his head. She did not shed a tear but simply asked the Wyandot with her to help carry the body to the waiting canoes and back across the river.

Thanks to Marie McIntosh, Lieutenant Muir was granted his dying wish, a proper Christian burial. But

Marie's life would never be the same. Never able to for-give herself for not reciprocating Muir's sentiments the day before he died, the young woman was robbed of her lighthearted ways and acquired a somber weight she would never be able to shed. For the rest of her life, she wore a black glove on the hand that Muir had touched, a constant reminder of the scar of guilt she bore.

As for Muir himself, for years afterwards, people spoke of a ghostly British officer drifting through the verdurous darkness of Mongaugon, near the Detroit River. He was said to appear once a year, on the evening of August 9. On this same day Marie McIntosh would make her yearly walk from Sandwich to Windsor, stop-ping at each house along the way to ask for money for the poor. So it was that the tragedy at Mongaugon left Marie looking for some sort of absolution and the ghost of Lieutenant Muir looking for some kind of peace. It is impossible to say whether or not they found what they were looking for. But given that Muir was never again seen on the banks of the Detroit after Marie finally passed on, the optimists among us may wish to assume that their story ended happily.

The Ghosts of Little Bighorn

"I always wanted to visit Little Bighorn," says Jason Davies (a pseudonym), a Vietnam War veteran who agrees to tell his story on condition of anonymity. "I mean I was raised on that 'How the West was Won,' stuff…John Wayne westerns and the like—and I guess I never really got over my childhood fascination for Custer's Last Stand." Jason pauses for a long moment on the telephone. "I probably thought I did for a while. When I got back from Vietnam, I kind of hit the ground running. Everything seemed so different when I got back, more serious. And it was a long, long time before I gave cowboys and Indians any thought again."

Ultimately, however, Davies realized that he hadn't lost his ardor for the story of the American frontier, but only put it aside for a while. "Years later, after my kids moved out and I put away my last paycheck, I started to go back to the Westerns. I got back into the movies. Every Friday, me and my wife rented two tapes; hers was always some big romantic thing, mine was always a Western. All I was reading was history books on the Old West. And then, in '98, when we were planning our seasonal holiday, it hit me. Hell, I'd never been to Little Bighorn." Davies managed to convince his wife that a road trip to Montana would be a lot of fun, and they left for the Little Bighorn Battlefield in late June, heading for the big skies and sweeping vistas of the famous western state.

They saw the same big skies and sweeping vistas that Custer and his Seventh Cavalry would have looked on in

1876, the year they were wiped out by thousands of Sioux and Cheyenne warriors on a nondescript hillock upon the plains of eastern Montana. There is little need to go over the details of the historic battle. Those readers unfamiliar with the particulars can read about the engagement in any one of the countless histories that have been written about it. Suffice to say that it was one of the great military disasters of American history, in which brash young Lieutenant Colonel George Armstrong Custer stumbled on his overconfidence. His disregard for the strength of his enemy compelled him to advance against an Indian war party when he should have waited for reinforcements and to divide his regiment into three separate battalions in the face of a larger enemy force. The outcome of Custer's strategy is well-known. On June 25, 1876, all 272 men of the Seventh Cavalry, including Custer himself, were attacked and killed.

This is all established historical fact, written and rewritten into the annals of the American narrative, enshrined in the national mythos. The supernatural legends that have long been associated with the battlefield, however, have not received nearly as much attention. Indeed, the shades, apparitions, inexplicable sounds and eerie sensations that so many witnesses have experienced on the battlefield over the years have largely been ignored by mainstream media.

And yet the stories persist. Passed on among paranormal enthusiasts from year to year, the accumulated reports of so many visitors' strange experiences have formed an alternative account of Little Bighorn. This account stands apart from the established themes of the official history.

For visitors to the Little Bighorn Battlefield National Monument who have had their visceral and jarring encounters with the site's supernatural denizens, the details of troop movements, the military lessons and social mores of the battlefield are distant footnotes.

What is the nature of these encounters? They are many and varied. Employees at the museum making their rounds after the doors are closed to the public have spotted a transparent likeness of Custer wandering among the artifacts. The description is always the same—he is dressed in full military regalia and is recognizable by his bushy handlebar mustache and sorrowful eyes. He never appears for longer than several seconds, taking a few paces, looking worried or pained, and then quickly fading to nothingness. Those who have seen Custer's apparition in the museum never recall it as a positive experience, for his ghost is always accompanied by a profound chill and a very real sense of dread. Park employees who have spotted Custer making his rounds attribute this oppressive feeling to the trauma of his demise and believe that his spirit still hasn't accepted his death and defeat.

The museum is not the only part of the battlefield believed to be haunted. Countless stories have emerged from residential apartments near the battlefield's cemetery. Tenants have spotted mist-shrouded apparitions of dead soldiers drifting down hallways. On other occasions, the dispossessed spirits have entered individuals' apartment suits. More than one tenant has woken in the middle of the night to find a transparent figure in 19th-century military dress standing at the foot of the bed, at the doorway or in the corner of the room.

The frequency of such sightings in private residences might suggest that the casualties of Little Bighorn are calling to the living for some sort of aid, attention or valediction. But for every ghost seen making itself at home in someone's apartment, there is at least one frazzled visitor who catches sight of a shimmering specter wandering aimlessly among the tombstones of the Little Bighorn cemetery.

Dressed in the same anachronistic military uniforms as the others, these phantoms appear most often at dusk, when the cemetery is nearly empty. The descriptions of the ghosts that appear in the graveyard at this time differ greatly. Some witnesses report seeing faint, barely visible apparitions concealed by patches of whirling mist, while others claim the images they saw appeared so lifelike that they assumed they were looking at historical reenactors or historical interpreters. That was until these "reenactors" abruptly vanished into thin air.

And then there are the goings-on at Reno's Crossing. Located some 5 miles from where Custer made his last stand, Reno's Crossing is the place where Major Marcus Reno waged his own foolhardy fight against a contingent of Indian braves on that fateful summer day in 1876. It was Reno who had actually initiated the battle, launching an attack on the enormous Indian camp near the Little Bighorn. But the Sioux counterattack that followed was so fierce that Reno and his troops were soon engaged in a desperate fighting withdrawal. They made their retreat through the deep ravines around the Little Bighorn River, holding their lines together for nearly two days.

Reno's Crossing is the place where Major Reno's men made their frantic dash across the Little Bighorn River under the withering fire of Indian rifles. Carrying or dragging what dead and wounded they could, the soldiers crossed the river and scrambled up the hills on the other side, where they dug in and made their own stand against the coming enemy. Unlike Custer and the cavalry under his command, Reno's unit survived the battle, though many of the major's men were killed in the fighting.

Today, Reno's Crossing is one of the attractions for history buffs visiting Little Bighorn, as well as for paranormal enthusiasts hoping to come face-to-face with a ghost from America's history. For of all the places on the famous battlefield where strange and inexplicable phenomena have occurred, Reno's Crossing is the place where they occur most often. Certainly Jason Davies would have something to say about this.

"I'm not sure how to put it," Davies says today. "The trip to the Little Bighorn Battlefield was nothing like I thought it would be. I mean, I knew everything about the battle when I went, and I guess I was expecting the ground where they fought to feel…I don't know…familiar." There is a long pause before Davies continues. "But the thing is, the moment my wife and I got out of the car at the National Monument, what I was most aware of was just how…*strange*…the place felt. It was everywhere, in the air. This *heaviness*. It was like nothing I'd ever felt before."

What was stranger to Davies was that his wife wasn't getting the same feeling. "I asked her about it. I asked her if there was anything about the place that spooked her out. She just looked at me like I was nuts, so I let it go." But the sense of foreboding didn't loosen its hold on Davies. In fact, it just got worse as the day went on.

"Things were weird at the cemetery, for sure. When I say weird, I mean…and this is gonna sound weird…that there were *others* there. And I don't mean other people that made the trip to see the battlefield." It wasn't long before Davies' intangible sense of foreboding took on more substantial manifestations.

"We were in the cemetery for just a few minutes when things started to get really spooky. You're going to think this is crazy." Davies hesitates for a moment. When he resumes, his voice is weighted with a somberness that wasn't there before. "I started hearing voices. They were men's voices; there was more than one…there was actually quite a few of them. All of them were speaking at the same time, and there were too many voices, all speaking way too softly for me to really make out what they were saying. But I'll tell you right now that none of these men were too happy about their situation."

As the sun sank farther under the horizon, the voices intensified, and Davies started to see moving shapes in his peripheral vision. "I was just standing there like some kind of zombie, floored by all of this stuff going on around me. I mean, first there were these guys, so many of these guys…whispering to me. Some of them were scared, others were angry and others were in pain. And then there were the shapes. I swore I saw them—men in dark uniforms, moving slowly towards me—out of the corner of my eyes. But whenever I turned to get a good look at them, they would vanish. There was nothing there."

Davies' wife walked ahead through the cemetery and didn't notice what was going on with her husband until she turned to tell him something about the cemetery. She was shocked at the sight of her husband, his ashen face frozen into an expression of terrified awe, his head swiveling toward some unseen wonder every few seconds. "I can only imagine what I must have looked like," Davies chuckles. "Because when my wife came up to me, the look on her face was like she had just snapped me out of a coma. She was worried and asked me what was wrong. I was going to ask her about the voices, took a look at her and decided that it might not be the best thing to do. So I tried to shrug the whole thing off and just told her something about how the cemetery jogged some memories about 'Nam."

That wouldn't be the end of the couple's experiences in Little Bighorn. "We ended up getting to the battlefield kind of late the first day," Davies says, "so we decided to save the rest of it for the next day. We walked through the museum there, went out to take a look at Last Stand Hill and then went out to Reno's Crossing." Davies is uncertain how to continue when he brings up the place where Marcus Reno's men made their retreat across the Little Bighorn River.

At first, he speaks haltingly. "Now in spite of everything I've told you," Davies begins, "I gotta tell you that I've never been one to think about ghosts or the afterlife or anything like that. It wasn't that I didn't believe; I just never got around to thinking about those sorts of things. And then the whole thing at Little Bighorn happened, and lately, it's all I've been able to think about. Especially after what I saw at Reno's Crossing."

The morning was warm and sunny. "Things felt better when we got up," Davies says. "They have an outstanding museum there, with more than enough to satisfy the historical enthusiast in me, and there wasn't a cloud in the

Visitors to the Little Bighorn Battlefield see and hear supernatural manifestations of the 1876 battle.

sky when he walked out to Last Stand Hill." The strange experience Jason Davies had in the cemetery the night before seemed a world away by the time they were making their way to Reno's Crossing. "I guess I just wanted to forget it. It was too weird. I mean, I'm not a kid anymore, you know? I'm soft in the middle. I wasn't ready to accept any big new revelations."

But like it or not, Jason Davies' worldview was about to change dramatically. "I remember that the sounds started almost the moment we were close enough to the Little Bighorn to hear its waters flowing. I'll always associate those sounds with that river. And when I think back, the rifle fire, shouts, screams and war whoops are inseparable from the sound of running water."

The sky may have been bright and clear, but once Jason and his wife were in the wooded ravines along the river, everything seemed to grow darker—just a tinge darker, but it made a world of difference to Jason. "It suddenly got cooler when we got close to the river, cooler and darker, and then the sounds started. They were faint at first," Davies says, "but they got louder with every step we took towards the river." If Jason was frightened at what he had witnessed the night before, his fear was infused with curiosity the next day. "I don't remember feeling nearly as much fear in Reno's Crossing as I did at the cemetery. More than anything else, I think I was curious, even excited."

It dawned on Jason Davies that he was coming into contact with much more American history at Little Bighorn than he ever thought he would. If the phenomena he was witnessing were indeed supernatural manifestations of the historical 1876 battle, then he wanted to see as much as he could. Davies ignored the goose bumps rising on the back of his neck and quickened his pace towards the river.

"On some instinctual level, I wanted to get out of there. My palms were sweaty, my heart was pounding and the adrenaline was pumping. It was like my body was telling me to turn around and run. And this time, I wasn't the only one that was feeling it." While Jason says that his wife didn't hear the sounds of battle the way he did, it was obvious that she was becoming uneasy as they approached the river. "Hell, who knows, to this very day, she won't talk about the Little Bighorn River, except to say that she just got a bad case of the 'creeps' when we walked up Reno's Crossing."

Jason Davies isn't so reticent about what he saw. "My heart stopped when we got to the river's edge. He was the first thing I saw. There, on the other side of the Little Bighorn, there was this soldier, an officer I think. He had red hair and a short red beard. He was just standing there in the trees, staring at me. I could tell right off that he was not real…or maybe I should say not *alive*, anyway. He looked really sad, like he was saying bye for good, and even though he didn't know who I was, he was still sad about it."

Davies can't say how long he stood there staring at the man on the other side of the river. "Sometimes when I think back to it, I'll think it might have been five minutes or so, but then other times I swear he was only there for a few seconds. My wife can't say either, 'cause she actually turned around before the riverbank and was waiting for me a few yards back. Well, however long it was, after he was done doing whatever he was doing, he vanished—there one second, gone the next. Just like that."

Davies and his wife returned home after spending one more day at the battlefield. Husband and wife have said very little to each other about what transpired on the Little Bighorn River. Mrs. Davies is just unwilling to talk about what it was that spooked her near Reno's Crossing, and Mr. Davies has no wish to aggravate his wife by bringing up the subject. And so Jason has kept the experience to himself for a few years now, not sure how friends and family would take it if he began ranting about phantom battles and the ghosts of soldiers who died over 100 years ago. "My kids already think I'm getting a bit strange in my old age," Davies jokes, "I throw info like this at 'em, they'd write me off all together."

One conversation with Jason Davies and it's clear that he isn't a befuddled old man but someone trying to come to grips with the incredible things he has experienced. Why did they appear to him and not to his wife? Did his time in Vietnam make him more likely to see the battlefield ghosts? But then why have other visitors, people who have never fought on a battlefield, had run-ins with the ghosts there? Indeed, why is it that some people see the ghosts and others do not? Are the spirits at Little Bighorn trying to say something? Or are they just lost souls still reeling from the trauma of their demise? These are questions that Davies might never find answers to, but his world has been changed because of them.

"Everything was different after our trip to Little Bighorn," Davies says. "It's been a few years now, but I still think about what I saw in Montana—about all those lost souls still roaming over the battlefield where they were killed. All my life, I've never been very religious, but since our trip in '98, I've taken to praying every now and then. I pray for my wife and my kids and myself and for all those men who were killed out on the Little Bighorn. I hope that one day, they find some peace."

The Phantom Rider of North Carolina

She was born bawling and screaming, but the moment the midwife placed her in Jenkins' arms, she was calm. She remained that way throughout her childhood. During these years, there was nothing in the world that could have driven a wedge between father and daughter. She was the apple of his eye, and she reciprocated his esteem with all the obedience and adoration that could be expected of any favorite child. But it did not last, and when the bond between this father and daughter broke, it was irreparably sundered.

Like so much in the United States at the time, the filial accord of the Jenkins family was consumed in the fires of the American Civil War. The seeds of their destruction were planted when the 16-year-old Jenkins girl got eyes for a young man who lived down Fletcher Road. It was a union Jenkins could never condone. Indeed, he swore he would die before allowing his one and only daughter to run off with the man she had chosen.

It is true that the world is full of fathers who hold reservations against their daughters' first love, but Jenkins had particular cause to frown on the boy his daughter had chosen. All his life, Jenkins had opposed the institution of slavery. Everything that grew on his farm had always been reaped and sowed with his own two hands, and he took pride in the fact that no slave had ever shed a drop of sweat on his property. As the question of slavery pushed the nation towards war, Jenkins became evermore vocal in his opposition to the Southern institution, and when the Civil War broke out, he was among Fletcher's firmest opponents to the Confederate cause.

Now it happened that Miss Jenkins' beau came from a family of well-known Confederate sympathizers. If this made things difficult between young Miss Jenkins and her fellow when the secession debates were raging across the country, it made their union impossible when the Civil War broke out. Soon after the first shots were fired on Fort Sumter, Jenkins forbade his daughter to see the young man down Fletcher Road. They continued to get together secretly, meeting beside the well at Calvary Episcopal Church. For years, local children called the water source outside Calvary Church a wishing well, where one need only take a draft from the well's water to have a wish granted.

It was at this wishing well that Jenkins' daughter accepted her beau's proposal soon after the war began. It was also at this wishing well, a few years into the war, that the young man told his fiancée he was going off to fight for the Confederacy. Their passion for one another had only grown during their long engagement, and the news was hard for the girl to bear. That day, before he marched off to join Braxton Bragg's army at Chattanooga, the Confederate soldier took a long drink from the waters of the wishing well and told his fiancée to do the same. They then made a wish together that whatever was to come, they would end up with one another, be it in this world or the next.

Life in the Jenkins household became unbearable after Miss Jenkins' fiancé went off to fight for the Confederacy. During the previous years, when she and her suitor were conducting their affair in secret, Miss Jenkins had kept quiet when her father embarked on one of his frequent tirades against the Confederacy. But now that her betrothed was actually in the fighting, she perceived her silence as some kind of betrayal. If her fiancé was confronting the bayonets of the enemy, she thought, surely she could confront her father.

So it was that the Civil War entered the Jenkins household, where nightly shouting matches over the dinner table always ended with mutual declarations of one another's infidelities. "You are a traitor to your family and your nation!" Jenkins would roar.

"And you are a traitor to our Southern boys!" his daughter would holler back before bolting from the table, out the house and to the well by Calvary Church, where she fervently prayed for the return of her fiancé.

Jenkins quickly put his daughter's recalcitrance together with the departure of the young man down Fletcher Road and confronted her about it during one of their dinnertime rows. "Don't think I don't know what's going on," he said, his voice dangerously low. "Your heart has gone to war along with that damn Rebel down the way. I can guess at what you two have promised each other, and I'll tell you now that you can forget about such foolishness. It will never happen. I won't permit it."

"It's too late!" the young woman screamed back. "We've already sworn to be married, and there's nothing you can do about it!" The constant fighting strained and then broke the bond between father and daughter. As the war turned from bad to worse for the Confederacy, Jenkins' daughter spent less and less time at home. She couldn't bear to look into the gloating eyes of her father and took refuge by the wishing well, where she drank big drafts and murmured heartbroken pleas into the air to be with her lover again.

The war was nearly over when word reached the town of Fletcher that the young woman's fiancé had been killed in battle. The news killed something in her heart and, once and for all, destroyed her relationship with her father. The last straw fell at the dinner table, when her father broke the silence with the hardest words he ever spoke. "Well now," he said between mouthfuls of biscuits and gravy, "looks like you won't be able to marry that boy after all, 'less you interested in having a wedding after the wake."

Overcome by grief, the Jenkins girl held on to life for a few more days before she passed away. Some of the more romantic interpretations of this legend say that she died of a broken heart, others that she poisoned herself. Whatever the case, she was found facedown next to the wishing well, with a strange and unsettling smile spread across her lifeless face. She was buried quickly and quietly after her death.

It is impossible to say what Jenkins felt at the death of his daughter. Whether it was anger, regret, grief, relief or a confused mess of all these, he was not given much time to dwell on the loss. For the very next evening after his daughter's funeral, Jenkins received a chilling visit from his deceased daughter—a visit that made it clear her death had resolved none of the issues between them.

She appeared at sunset. The Jenkins family was on the veranda of the farmhouse. It was a quiet, somber night, and they sat staring at the sky as the sun slowly sank out of sight, lost in their own thoughts, when the wind picked up. It was a cool breeze, welcome at first, which broke the heat of the early fall night. It started as a murmur among the pine trees of Calvary Church, and the cool it brought was a relief. Jenkins' wife smiled at turned her face towards it. "Thank God," she said.

The moment the words were out of her mouth, the wind picked up an ominous force. The church bells swayed and chimed weakly under the powerful gusts. The pine trees at Calvary swayed and trembled as the sun dropped out of sight and the sky quickly darkened. In the semi-darkness of dusk she came. At first, the Jenkins family didn't know who it was but could only stare in awe at the approaching figure. She was mounted atop a tall palomino horse moving at full gallop, flying down Fletcher Road at an impossible speed.

The first thing Jenkins recognized was the horse. Even as his eyes took in the sight of the familiar animal—the same horse that belonged to the young Confederate whom his daughter had fallen in love with—he refused to believe it. And then he was able to make out the rider. The sight of her was like an ice-cold hand fastening around his heart and squeezing. It was his daughter, or something that used to be his daughter. Her sallow face was stripped of the sanguine blush that once colored her cheeks and lips and was drawn into an expression of such gravity that she was almost unrecognizable to her own family. She wore a gray Confederate coat around her shoulders—the coat of her fiancé. She pulled up her horse when she reached her father's farmhouse. The ground the horse stood upon showed no signs of her passing, but a shifting cloud of mist hung around the animal's flanks. Jenkins and his family were dumbstruck.

An eternity seemed to pass before a hollow, inhuman voice passed through her colorless lips. "Father, I might have been a happy wife, but your anger and your politics left no room for a happy daughter. Now I will ride a dead horse on a cold wind forever. This is my fate." Jenkins began to quietly sob. He tried to form an apology, but to apologize to such a lifeless, terrible thing suddenly struck him as absurd.

"I will never forget your hate for the man I loved, nor your loyalty for the North. I will make sure you are rewarded for both."

"What do you mean to do to us?" it was her mother who spoke.

Jenkins' daughter did not take her expressionless eyes off her father. "Next spring, an army from the North will come. They will come with victory and with fire. But you, father, will not have cause to celebrate, because they will think you a Confederate and burn your farm to the ground. I promise you this will occur."

Jenkins began to stammer his protest, but before he could get a single word out, the ghost of his daughter turned and galloped away on her beau's phantom steed, riding on to Fletcher Road and vanishing in a flash.

Jenkins would never live to see the prophecy realized. A heavy veil fell over the Jenkins family after that day, and one by one, all the Jenkins children moved out, the workers that helped on the farm quit and friends stopped calling. Jenkins' wife died early that winter, and Jenkins himself died shortly after, carrying his sorrow and regret to the grave. The house itself was left unoccupied, and that coming spring, Union troops arrived.

They had no way of knowing that Jenkins had been firmly pro-Unionist while he lived, and events leading up to their arrival in Fletcher led them to believe that the abandoned farmhouse was being used a Confederate base. All the way up Fletcher Road, General Stoneman's troops were being harassed by a mysterious Confederate rider on a palomino horse. It began when his column had been lured into an ambush a few miles down the road. They had been marching up the road when the rider burst out of the surrounding trees, faced the soldiers at the front of the column and reared his horse up on its two hind legs, as if to challenge the Union advance.

The commanding officer of the Union's vanguard was a major, and he immediately gave the order to fire. A handful of men let out a volley, but the horseman remained miraculously unscathed, though several bullet holes now appeared in his gray cloak. The rider then turned and galloped down the road with incredible speed. The major gave the order to pursue, and the men eagerly charged after the rider. Not 50 yards down Fletcher Road from where they had encountered the lone rider, the Union column was ambushed by waiting Confederates. Stoneman's men quickly dealt with the

Confederate guerrillas, but throughout the fight, no one saw any trace of the horseman who had led them into the trap.

After the ambush, General Stoneman moved to the front of the column and took charge of the forward units himself. They resumed their march up the road, but they didn't go far before they spotted the Confederate rider again, sitting absolutely still in the heavy shade of the surrounding forest. It was too dark to make out his features, but the major recognized the great palomino horse and the bullet-ridden gray cloak and told General Stoneman that this was their man.

Cautious about making the same mistake twice, the general sent scouts ahead to comb the area for Confederate guerillas. The mysterious rider galloped out of sight before the approaching scouts, leaving them to do their work in peace. After a thorough search of the entire area, the scouts found no trace of any Confederate soldiers. "That bastard is playing around with us," General Stoneman grumbled before giving the order to resume the march.

That wouldn't be the last time they saw the Confederate rider. They had been marching for the better part of an hour after last spotting the rider when he burst from the trees a mere 20 yards away, crashing through the forest and onto the middle of the road, where, once again, he reared his horse onto its hind legs in a brazen challenge. For an instant, General Stoneman and his soldiers were only able to look on in shock at this suicidal stunt. The first question on Stoneman's mind was how this rider managed to get past the web of scouts that he now had spread out before the bulk of his force. The second question was how any man could be so foolhardy—appearing no more than 20 yards in front of a force just after leading that same force into an ambush!

"Kill the Rebel bastard!" General Stoneman roared, and the sound of gunfire drowned out the tail end of his order. A strange silence followed as the men peered through the thick cloud of gun smoke that obscured the trail. Not one of the soldiers actually expected to see the rider standing, but there wasn't a man there so sure of the fact that he would step forward to take a closer look.

They would not have to. With the swiftness of a scythe stroke, a strong and bone-chilling wind blew over Fletcher Road, causing the hair on every soldiers' neck to stand on end and the haze of smoke and powder to curl away in frightened tendrils. No one dared to believe his eyes. He was still there, sitting atop his horse and shrouded in the forest's shade—unscathed.

General Stoneman snapped. Roaring in rage, the general unholstered his revolver, aimed at his enemy and fired, sending a bullet tearing into a tree right behind where the horseman sat. Unaffected, the rider wheeled around and bolted away with remarkable speed. General Stoneman gave chase, yelling at the top of his voice and emptying his revolver at the rapidly vanishing horseman. The horse was galloping so fast that the advance scouts ahead of the Union troops didn't have enough time to raise their rifles to their shoulders before horse and rider tore past.

General Stoneman was equal parts bewilderment, rage and awe. Not able to understand how he could have missed the rider six times, he was also fuming at the rider's ability to twice escape what should have been certain death. He fulminated against his soldiers, cursing every man in his path, but this was the show he put on to hide the fear rising within. *How could anything move that fast?* he thought to himself, recalling the speed with which the rider galloped away. *No living thing can move that fast.*

The next time the soldiers saw the rider, however, they were the ones who got the jump on him. Advanced scouts spied the distinctive palomino when they crept up to the boundary of the Jenkins farmhouse. The rider was still mounted on the horse, standing in total stillness, staring intently at the empty veranda.

The lead scout, a sergeant, whispered his order. "Go tell the general we've got our Reb."

The message was quickly relayed back to General Stoneman. "We've got 'im sir," a breathless scout reported. "He's sittin' still outside a farmhouse not 300 yards down the road."

The general ordered his column to halt and then accompanied the soldier back up the road to the other scouts. They were hidden in the woods just beyond the edge of the farm, silently surveying the rider that had given them so much trouble. "How long has he been standing there?" General Stoneman whispered to the sergeant, looking at the lone figure with wonder.

"Can't say, sir. He's circled the house a few times, but he's always come back to the front."

"Anybody in the house?" the general asked.

"We haven't seen anyone, no sir."

General Stoneman studied the Jenkins farmhouse and the horseman for a long moment. "I want your best shot on that man, sergeant. Take him down. After he's dead, we fire the house."

The whispered order went down the line. A sharpshooter came crawling up a few moments later. He wasn't much more than 20 years old, and he gulped hard when he saw that he was in the presence of a general. "Yes, sir?"

He addressed the sergeant, but it was the general who spoke. "You see that man standing by the farmhouse?"

The sharpshooter nodded.

"I want you to kill him. Do you think you can do that?"

The sharpshooter had made far more difficult shots, and he couldn't keep the smile from creeping to his face. "Shucks, sir, there won't be anything to it."

"Good." The general held his breath as the young private leveled his rifle at his target. Looking down the barrel of his Enfield, the sharpshooter took one long look at the back of the rider's head before squeezing the trigger. But instead of falling dead off his horse, the rider wheeled around to face the smoking rifle barrel. General Stoneman leapt to his feet. "Shoot that rider down!" he yelled at every scout hidden along the clearing.

The woods came to life with gunfire as every man with anything to shoot opened up on the galloping figure, but the mysterious Confederate got away again, leaving a forest full of stunned Union soldiers. "But I got 'im," the sharpshooter said, pleading to no one in particular. "I swear to God I got 'im."

General Stoneman turned his back on the old Jenkins farmhouse. "Sergeant! I believe this farm belongs to

Confederate sympathizers. I want you to fire the house and every other building that stands on this land. Burn them all to the ground."

And so it was that the Jenkins girl's prophecy had come to pass. Her father's farm was razed by Union soldiers who believed it was the property of Confederate sympathizers. While Jenkins wasn't alive to witness the ironic destruction of his home, General Stoneman himself came to realize that he might have been acting as a pawn in a larger drama.

The realization came the very same night he ordered the destruction of the farm. He and his troops were camped near Calvary Church, but Stoneman was far too restless to sleep. The events of the day kept replaying in his mind, and General Stoneman gave up on sleeping some time past midnight. He got out of bed and took a walk through the churchyard, mulling over the details of the day. How could he have fired an entire revolver at the horseman and miss every time? On three separate occasions, the rider had come under fire from an entire line of riflemen, only to get away unhurt each time. The young sharpshooter was so stunned by the fact that he missed his target that he refused to believe it. "I killed that man, sir," he heard the sniper telling his sergeant. "I shot him through the head. He's dead." But he was not dead. The Confederate got away again. And how quickly the rider was able to get away. He swore that in all his years, he had never seen any living thing move as fast as that horse.

General Stoneman stopped at the Calvary Church wishing well. *No man is that lucky,* he thought to himself. No man could evade near certain death five times in one day. Maybe not—but what about a woman? Or more accurately, what about the ghost of a woman, bent on revenge?

The general was standing listlessly in front of the wishing well when a cold wind swept through the churchyard. In the next instant, he was standing face-to-face with his enemy. Animal and master came darting out of the darkness so suddenly that Stoneman wasn't sure whether to believe his eyes for a second or two. Then he registered the palomino horse, the gray bullet-ridden cloak. He was standing close enough to strike the rider down with a saber, but his pistol and sword were back in his tent. He stood there unarmed, at the mercy of the soldier he had tried so hard to kill that day. Slowly, his gaze moved up to the face of the rider, and when he saw who was sitting atop the animal, his mind reeled in fear and confusion.

Her hair was pitch black and her skin bore the ghastly pallor of a corpse. She sat still as a statue, staring down at the awestruck general with a blank expression, and in that moment Stoneman realized that he could see the starry sky behind her. She was transparent. It dawned on him then. He and his men weren't able to kill this rider because she was already dead! They had been shooting at a ghost. But he didn't know what she wanted with his men. He didn't understand why she had led them to the farmhouse. In fact, he had no idea why she was here now, staring at him with her lifeless eyes. The general was still staring in mute incomprehension when he was struck by the feeling that she wasn't looking *at* him, but *through* him.

Casting a glance over his shoulder, the general remembered that he was standing in front of the wishing well. He stepped aside, so she was able to see it. The moment her eyes fell on the church well, they softened and something like a smile crept into the corners of her pallid lips. And then she was gone, galloping out of the Union camp so quickly that the sentries weren't able to raise their rifles fast enough to fire at her.

Though the ghost of the Jenkins girl had seen her father's farm burn to the ground, she did not stop riding Fletcher Road after her prophecy had been realized. She told her father that she was doomed to ride a dead horse on a cold wind forever, and it seems as if forever is what she meant. For to this very day, a speeding rider is often seen tearing up Fletcher Road at night, seated atop a palomino horse, a gray cloak perforated with bullet holes streaming behind it. Those who have gotten closer looks at this phantom rider note her black hair, her pale skin and the strange emotionless determination on her face. But they are never able to look for long. She rides as fast as the cold wind that precedes her and vanishes as quickly as she appears—eternally riding for whatever place she is cursed to never reach.

The Beauregard-Keyes House

This story is also found in Ghost Stories of the Civil War, *which I co-wrote with Edrick Thay (Ghost House Books, 2003) –DA*

The violence of Civil War battles was a terrible thing to behold. Whenever North met South on battlefields across the country, the roaring machinery of death came to life with an awful force, unprecedented in the annals of military history. Cannon rained down on enemy positions over great distances. Soldiers were blown apart by 6-, 10- and 12-pound balls of lead that flew across contested territory. Rows of riflemen carried Springfield and Enfield rifles that were accurate to nearly half a mile away; their fire swept over approaching columns like an invisible scythe. While soldiers of the Civil War were subjected to all sorts of awful advances in technology, the generals continued to conduct their fights as generals had for over a century. Particularly instructed by the study of Napoleonic military tactics, Civil War officers—Union and Confederate—took strategies out of books that were written when the weapons of war weren't nearly as effective.

And so it was that entire regiments of men were ordered to march across open ground, just as their predecessors who fought over Europe half a century before had, holding rigid marching formations as they were ripped apart by crashing cannon and withering rifle fire. Casualties were not only heavy but highly visible and exceedingly gruesome. Civil War battles were brazen expositions of the worst humanity was capable of, and few who survived them would ever be the same. Yet given the brutality of this style of fighting, there has been surprisingly little written about the effects of the fighting on the minds of the men who fought. Surprising because we have gotten so used to hearing about the troubles that plague fighting men after they are exposed to the horrors of war. Post–Traumatic Stress Disorder was first diagnosed among veterans who were having difficulties coping with everyday life after their experiences in the jungles of Vietnam. In World War I, it was called "shell shock," in World War II, "combat fatigue." Yet even as society has acknowledged these casualties in every military conflict of the 20th century, very little has been said of the shell-shocked Civil War veterans. How did the men who survived the horror of a Gettysburg, an Antietam or a Shiloh cope with the world after they fulfilled their duties?

Only recently has any historical research been done on the mental trauma of Civil War veterans. The latest studies do indeed suggest that a good number of men had difficulty coming to terms with their experiences. Certainly, anybody witnessing the strange goings-on in the famous Beauregard-Keyes House in New Orleans might get the impression that at least one Civil War soldier was struggling with the horror of the things he had seen on the field of battle.

Pierre Gustave Toutant Beauregard was one of the premier generals of the Confederate army. The native Louisianan showed great promise at West Point, graduating

Did the trauma of the Civil War cause Pierre Beauregard to haunt his former home?

second in his class. Later he rose to military prominence during the Mexican War and was appointed superintendent of West Point just months before the Civil War broke out. Beauregard was a stern and competent officer whose pride in his Southern roots equaled his military reputation, so no one was surprised when he made the decision to pitch in with the Confederate cause.

It was actually General Beauregard who was responsible for the opening shots of the Civil War, as he ordered the bombardment of Fort Sumter on April 13, 1861. The Southern papers made the acclaimed "Hero of Fort Sumter" into something of a celebrity, and a few months later, he commanded the Confederate Army of the Potomac to victory during the First Bull Run. Dubbed "Little Napoleon" by his military peers for his admiration of Napoleon Bonaparte, after Bull Run, the Creole general might have dared to dream of a legacy comparable to that of his martial hero. If he did entertain any such fantasies of military glory, they were quashed in early April 1862, when Beauregard took command of the Confederate forces during the Battle of Shiloh.

The first major engagement in the Civil War's western theater, Shiloh saw the meeting of 65,000 Union soldiers with roughly 44,000 Confederates on the west bank of the Tennessee River over April 6 and 7. It was a bloody two-day seesaw of attack and counterattack, and when the smoke cleared over the contested ground, there were over 24,000 dead, wounded and missing, with the Union forces standing over the field. Beauregard's first loss was a major blow to the Confederacy. The Union victory at Shiloh led to the occupation of Corinth, Mississippi, a major railroad hub for the Confederacy and a key strategic location.

By all accounts, General Beauregard had difficulty dealing with what he experienced at Shiloh. Shortly after retreating from Corinth, the "Little Napoleon" went on a

The Beauregard-Keyes House in New Orleans was home to a Confederate general—in his life and afterlife.

sick leave for over two months without Jefferson Davis' permission. The Confederate president was outraged at the Creole general's insubordination and ordered that Beauregard be permanently stripped of his military rank. By September of that year, a shortage of skilled officers saw Davis rescinding his order, and Beauregard was rein-stated to a military command. Beauregard served the Confederate army for the duration of the Civil War but would never live up to the promise of his first months.

Resigning to civilian life after the Confederate defeat, Beauregard went on to become one of New Orleans' lead-ing citizens, making a tidy sum in railroad development and serving a term as Louisiana's adjutant general. But despite his post-war affluence, there is reason to believe Beauregard had some difficulty leaving the war behind him—especially the Battle of Shiloh. Indeed, the strange and inexplicable experiences of many of those who have visited the Beauregard-Keyes House in New Orleans' French Quarter have led them to believe that what the general saw at the critical Tennessee battle left a deep and lasting mark on his psyche. Beauregard lived in the stately old mansion that bares his namesake for only one year, from 1865 to 1866. A short time, yes, but apparently it was a time in his life that he would never forget, a time that was loaded heavily with tortured memories of the first battle the general lost.

The stories about the Beauregard-Keyes House begin in 1893, the same year the general passed away. It was in that year that people walking by Beauregard's former residence late at night first heard the voice. The voice was old and raspy, and in a tone that landed somewhere between horror and regret it spoke "Shiloh…Shiloh" over and over again.

None who heard the mournful mantra believed it came from anyone, or anything, that lived. It was dis-tinctly unnatural, a voice barely above a whisper that somehow seemed to come from a very great distance. It was as if a man somewhere inside the darkened house lost in a nightmare was muttering the object of his dread over and over in a fitful sleep. And yet passersby walking by the house were able to hear the terrified whispers as if the sleeping man was lying right next to them, somehow conveying his terror on all who heard the two tortured syllables. Many who heard the name of the Civil War battle found themselves running away from the Beauregard-Keyes House as fast as their legs could carry them.

It didn't take long for people to link the whispering voice to the former resident who lost the battle whose name was being whispered. The assumption that some postmortem remnant of General Beauregard still resided in the New Orleans mansion gained currency when house residents began to talk of a semi-transparent apparition that appeared in the ballroom in the middle of the night. According to witnesses, the shimmering figure was dressed in a Confederate gray military uniform and bore a striking resemblance to photographs of Beauregard as he appeared in the prime of his life. Most people who saw the general standing in the ballroom did not stand around gaping for too long. The sight of Beauregard was often accompanied by a severe temperature drop that chilled witnesses to the bone. Some who saw the general claimed that they were moved by an almost instinctual drive to turn around and run, sensing, on one level or another, that the figure standing in front of them was a ghostly expression of pure misery.

Luckily for those living in the Beauregard-Keyes House, the ghost of General Beauregard did not stay in the

On the other side of this door in the Beauregard-Keyes House, disturbing phantom renditions of the Battle of Shiloh play out.

ballroom for too long. It is not known exactly when he stopped appearing, but within one year, reports of run-ins with Beauregard's ghost stopped. Yet whatever relief residents of the mansion may have felt was short-lived, for soon after Beauregard's spirit ceased its loitering in the ballroom, another equally disturbing phenomenon began. That was when the general and his solitary cry for the battle he lost was replaced by a supernatural manifestation of the battle itself—when the ballroom transformed before startled witnesses' eyes into a ghostly Shiloh, complete with bugles, drums, rifles, artillery and casualties.

The cacophony of battle was heard only late in the evening, and like Beauregard's whisper, somehow sounded very far and very near at the same time. Anyone woken by the sound of battle late at night could follow the ruckus down to the ballroom, where, according to legend, they were in for quite a sight.

There, instead of the Beauregard-Keyes ballroom, was a sort of phantom rendition of the Battle of Shiloh. Those who witnessed it told of rows of weary-looking men standing in a surreal landscape dotted by vague visions of trees, river and hills. Some likened the sight to an impressionist painting, others to some bizarre dreamscape. The men standing in their stolid rows—soldiers from the North and the South—did not actually fight but remained deathly still, staring ahead expressionless as the muted sound of battle boomed and cracked through the erstwhile ballroom. Long moments would pass, during which most witnesses, awestruck or frightened, believed that they were looking upon some sort of supernatural roll call, until they realized that, one by one, the soldiers in front of them were taking injuries. It happened with every crash of cannon and fusillade of rifle fire: one member of the phantom troop would suddenly be perforated through the chest, another would lose an arm, yet another would have his leg blown off and crumple to the ground. And still they remained there, the dead of Shiloh, staring ahead in silence even as they were being cut down by the distant sounds of rifle and cannon.

Many who have witnessed the haunting in the ballroom turn and run before the ghostly battle has run its course, while those possessed more by curiosity than by fear stand and watch until each soldier is struck down. It is then that a speedy decomposition begins, as the visage of every fallen soldier rapidly changes into a grinning skull, and the cuts and lacerations of wounded limbs fade into clean bone. And then they are gone. The end of the supernatural scene always ends in the same way, concluding the moment the morning sun rises over New Orleans. That is when the skeletal apparitions gradually fade into nothingness and the hills and trees of the ghostly Shiloh are replaced by the furnishings of the Beauregard-Keyes ballroom. By the time the sun has risen, not a trace of the supernatural battle remains.

Unlike the ghost of General Beauregard, the phantom battle has continued to be reported throughout the years. Just as subsequent owners spoke of the strange sights and sounds in the ballroom, reports of the phenomenon continued for years, even after the doors of the Beauregard-Keyes House were opened to the public when the mansion was made into a National Historic Site. Passersby late at night will still talk about hearing sounds of battle coming from within. And despite statements by the house's caretakers that they have never seen anything out of the ordinary in the ballroom, the house curators have acknowledged that there is something about the house that frightens them. Many paranormal enthusiasts and investigators consider the house to be one of New Orleans' premier haunted sites.

It is interesting that the ghost of General Beauregard stopped appearing after so short a time, while the ghostly vision of Shiloh, his greatest defeat, continues to be reported today, over 100 years later. Could this be evidence of how deeply the Louisianan general was affected by what he experienced on the Tennessee battlefield? Perhaps Beauregard was more sensitive than history gives him credit for, and suffered greatly for the horror he saw on April 6 and 7, 1862. He lived in the Beauregard-Keyes House for only one year after the Civil War, but could it be that the memory of the battle was so intense that he could not get himself to forget? Could he have wandered down to the ballroom in the middle of sleepless nights, where—in the same feverish delirium experienced by so many other veterans who lived through horrific battles—he relived the details of those two terrible days night after night after night? Can it be that these flashbacks were so intense that they left some sort of psychic residue in the ballroom that is still felt today? That would mean that the ghosts haunting the Beauregard-Keyes House are not the ghosts of the soldiers who died at Shiloh, but the ghosts of General Beauregard's nightmares—the remnants of one man's struggles with the horrors of the Civil War.

The Ghosts of 1812

Chances are that if there's a haunting in Toronto or the greater area of southern Ontario, Matthew Didier will know something about it. And if not, drop him a line and tell him about it, as he's sure to be interested. Born and raised in the grand old city of Toronto, Ontario, Didier is a man who is serious about the pursuit of the unknown. So serious, in fact, that in 1997, he established GHRS, The Ghosts and Hauntings Research Society, an organization defined by a mission to investigate ghosts and "the history, legends, myths and firsthand accounts" that pertain to them. Since then, Didier's integrity, rigorous investigative methodology and tireless diligence have made the GHRS into one of Canada's largest and most respected supernatural investigators, spawning 14 regional chapters across Canada, the United States and into the United Kingdom.

But Didier's primary focus remains trained on paranormal phenomena that occur in southern Ontario. It has been a pursuit that has kept Didier very busy over the years and given him a thorough knowledge of Toronto and its surrounding area. One conversation with Matthew Didier and one is struck by how well he knows his home—as it is today and as it was in the past.

Indeed, it seems that Matthew's fascination with ghosts feeds directly into his fascination for history, and as it turns out, he's something of a military history buff, who has been a keen participant in more than one battlefield reenactment. Battlefield reenactor and paranormal investigator—there could hardly be a better person to talk to about this book.

On the phone, it quickly becomes obvious that Didier's interests in military history and hauntings are not mutually exclusive. "There's some pretty traumatic history wrapped up in the battlefields around here," Didier says, "which is bound to lead to some ghost stories." Trauma— this is the most prevalent theory about ghosts, that just like the living, the dead are prone to relive any trauma they may have experienced, especially if the trauma occurred in the last moments of their lives. Is it any wonder, then, that ghostly soldiers are said to be crawling all over southern Ontario, where so much of the fighting in the War of 1812 occurred? Not according to Matthew Didier, who states that there are enough ghostly tales centered on this war's engagements to cover a whole chapter.

Yet if an entire chapter on the big 1812 battlefields would be unfair attention to the this one war, there is certainly room enough for two tales. These are two tales that, among Ontario paranormal enthusiasts, might be considered long-established folklore, and, for many bewildered eyewitnesses, are strange and unsettling experiences, not easily forgotten.

THE BATTLE OF CHIPPEWA

If the War of 1812 is the great forgotten war, then Chippewa is its invisible battlefield. Matthew Didier boils this down to Canadian nationalism. "The interesting thing about Chippewa," Matthew says, "is because it wasn't a Canadian victory, it wasn't really celebrated and was a farmer's field for basically 200 years." It's easy to see why the nation would prefer to forget Chippewa, given the rather embarrassing details of the battle.

The battle took place on July 5, 1814, when roughly 7000 British soldiers under Major General Sir Phineas Riall mistook a troop of gray-clad Americans led by General Winfield Scott for militia. General Riall, suffering from that particular kind of arrogance that British officers were so often afflicted by, boldly ordered his men across the Chippewa River to engage the approaching enemy. As it turned out, General Scott's men weren't militia, but sturdy regulars who were well trained, able to execute any battlefield command, weather a rifle barrage and charge with the bayonet as well as any British fighting man.

Riall, however, was expecting more of the same rag-tag American militia he had been fighting against in the war thus far and made his impetuous crossing of the Chippewa assuming that the Americans would scatter at the first shot of artillery. Of course, that is not what happened. And it was when the American soldiers took the worst the British could deliver and handed it right back that General Riall was to famously exclaim, "Those are regulars, by God!" Regulars who would outmaneuver, outfight and, in the end, outlast the British that day. By the time the last gun fell silent on the Chippewa battlefield, it was the Americans who were standing over the field, with some 330 casualties, while the British slinked from the battlefield after suffering over 600 dead, wounded or captured. The Americans buried their dead enemies on the field where they fell.

If Chippewa was a source of some pride for the American military, after the War of 1812 was over, the battlefield lay within Canadian borders, and Canada did nothing to commemorate the defeat. Years turned to decades, which turned to centuries, and the mortal drama that played itself out on the Chippewa battlefield was buried under the passage of time and the farmer's plow.

Until, that is, very recently. According to Matthew Didier, only in the last four years has the battlefield been reclaimed as a place of national import, where a memorial, a plaque and about an acre and a half of grassland has been set aside to commemorate the fighting. Before that, the Chippewa battlefield was essentially farmland. "When we made our first trip to Chippewa to investigate some stories we heard, we kind of just stumbled on it," Didier says.

What kind of tips was Didier's group going to check out? "There were two different sources," Didier says today. "One of them was a group of guys that were out there one night, around dusk, firing off .22s. The battlefield wasn't marked back then, but they described the area to us, the location, and we were able to confirm that it was Chippewa." Whatever shenanigans these kids were up to, they came to an abrupt end when the sounds of carnage became audible—carnage that was impossible with just a couple of loaded .22s. "They heard a battle being fought around them," Didier says. "They heard cannon shots, rifle shots, men screaming. At first, they assumed that it was just some kind of reenactment in a fort nearby, but then it just faded away as quickly as it came."

While one such report might not necessarily merit an investigation, two certainly would, and Didier's organization received another call about Chippewa not long after the first. "The other call was these two guys who were out hiking around the area. It was about the same time of day—dusk—and they were walking around the battlefield when they heard the same thing, the sounds of battle." Just as with the gun-toting witnesses, the pair heard the sound of rifle fire and artillery, the shouts of combatants, the screams of the dying. The sound came out of nowhere, lasted for a few moments and then faded away, leaving the pair standing in the field, wondering whether or not to believe their ears. In the end, they must have concluded that they had indeed heard what they had heard, because they gave Didier's organization a call.

The GHRS investigation ended up yielding very little, cut short by authorities concerned that Didier's group was intending to dig up the buried soldiers. Though Didier assured them that they carried only recording devices, not digging tools, the investigation was aborted and has never been resumed. Nevertheless, the following years brought some good news for Didier and other 1812 military enthusiasts, as the Chippewa battlefield received some formal recognition, allowing for the first ever Chippewa battle reenactment to take place in the summer of 2004.

FORT YORK

The ghosts of Fort York find their origins in yet another losing battle for British and Canadian forces. The fort was attacked three times by the Americans in the War of 1812, and occupied two of the three times. The first attack on the fort was by far the bloodiest. In April 1813, an American force under the command of Brigadier General Zebulon Pike landed on Sunnyside Beach, just north of Fort York. A force of 119 grenadiers was sent out to meet the attackers, but Zebulon's well-covered skirmishers promptly cut the proud grenadiers, who marched in their rigid battlefield formation across open ground. It was a massacre. By the time the grenadiers sounded the retreat, only 30 men were able to limp back to the safety of Fort York.

Little did these men know that no succor was to be found in the fort. The rest of the British garrison at York, under the command of Major General Roger Hill Sheaff, decided that the fight was a lost cause and withdrew before the retreating grenadiers and advancing Americans. They made sure to leave a nasty surprise behind for the Americans. Unbeknownst to the approaching men, the British had lit a fuse in the fort's main powder magazine to prevent it from falling into American hands. The military protocol at the time dictated that any army abandoning a fort lower its flag upon vacating, but at York, Sheaff left the colors fluttering in the wind as the garrison withdrew. The approaching soldiers, under the impression Fort York was still manned, had no way of knowing that a burning fuse was about to send the whole place up.

"Other than the Halifax explosion, this was the next largest explosion in Canadian history," Didier says. "People said they saw it, heard it, felt it, as far away as Richmond Hill." For the men near the fort, the aftermath was horrific. The grenadiers retreating to the fort, along with Canadian militia in the region and the approaching Americans, suffered terribly. Hundreds of soldiers died.

General Pike, considered one of the most promising military men in the American army, was killed by a piece of flying debris from the explosion.

But the suffering did not end here. The Americans, livid at the surprise firing of the fort, took their rage out on the wounded British and Canadians who were left behind. Gathering the enemy casualties together, they locked them in all in the fort's one surviving blockhouse for over 24 hours, without food, water or medical attention. It took the fury of Reverend John Strachan to convince the Americans to open the blockhouse and allow the wounded the care that was their right—but by then, much of the damage was already done.

Is it any wonder that so much suffering in one place might leave a supernatural imprint behind? Didier's GHRS needed little prompting to conduct their own investigations of Historic Fort York. Between the GHRS's investigations and numerous reports they've received from reliable sources, there's reason to believe the old fort houses many spirits unable to come to terms with their terrible ends.

The doors at Fort York seem to have some significance to the ghosts there. "We've been to the fort a number of times," Didier says, "and one occasion I saw the latch on the door to the officer's quarters move on its own. We went to check it out, and there was no one there."

Didier recalls another door-related phenomenon: "We also have another firsthand account from a fellow who works there, who told us about the center blockhouse door, that it slammed shut while he was walking by it a few times—slammed shut hard. The thing about this door is that we tried to mimic how it might have closed when he told us about it, and it's heavy. You've got to put all of your weight into it just to get it to move. But it just slammed shut on him."

Slamming doors and wiggling latches aren't the only things that occur at the fort. "I have one city of Toronto worker on file talking about what she saw one night when she was closing up," Didier says. "She's shutting down and she notices that in the officers' quarters there's a light. So she figures that she's left the light on, and goes to turn it off, but as she gets closer, she sees figures in the quarters' dining room area. And as she got closer she realized that there was an entire dinner going on. Well," Didier continues," she said that she took a few more steps, as curious as you'd expect anyone to be, but then the figures progressively faded." By the time this woman got to the quarters, there was no on there.

If there truly are spectral officers still manning their posts at Fort York, they're evidently still looking out for their brothers in arms. "Here's an account that happened to a friend of mine in the Royal Regiment of Canada in the 1980s," Didier continues. "Now they meet in the Fort York Armory, which is right next to the old fort. One of the fellows in the regiment used to like to jog around Old Fort York on top of the earthworks. So apparently, one day, he's rounding the southeast corner and he felt someone grab him by the thigh and pull him down into the fort."

"Now this guy was [really angry]," Didier continues. "He figured that it was somebody pulling a stupid prank, and thinking that he could have easily gotten hurt, he turned around ready to pop the guy that grabbed him. No one there." The frazzled soldier, now too alarmed and distracted to continue his run, made his way back to the armory, not sure what to make of what he had just experienced. "Now, according to my source, who was there at the time," Didier states, "this guy came in and told everyone what had happened. That was when they all noticed this handprint on this guy's thigh—this white mark of a hand that grabbed him real hard."

While Matthew Didier's friend couldn't think of any explanation as to how or why this would have happened, Didier himself is forthcoming with an explanation. "A popular theory about ghosts is that they don't know they're dead—they still think that they're existing in the time they [died]. So imagine if you're one of the militia guys, stuck in the fort, you don't know it's about to explode, all you see around you is Americans...it isn't good. And then you see this loon, on the walls, running in the line of fire. For all we know, this ghost may have thought that he was helping this soldier out—pulling him down out of harm's way."

If this is indeed the case, though Americans are no longer besieging Toronto and centuries divide these brothers in arms, at least the phantom behind the walls of Old Fort York is aiding a soldier of the same army.

Defeat at Ball's Bluff

Everything seemed to change the day the grotesque flotilla of dead Union soldiers arrived in Washington, D.C., borne through the country's capital on the gentle waters of the Potomac. There were dozens of them, floating downriver in terrifying repose, their blue uniforms creased and water blackened, lifeless grimaces on their bone white faces. They were only a few dozen dead in a war that would claim hundreds of thousands, but the news of their approach sent a spasm of fear through Washington, D.C. It was late October 1861, the Civil War had just begun and the public was still adjusting to the idea of casualties. Few people in Washington were ready to deal with the consequences of war, let alone stare them in the face as they floated by. Those bodies not intercepted by fishermen eventually washed ashore in the nation's capital; except, that is, for a single bloated corpse that floated straight through Washington, continuing downstream before being deposited on Mount Vernon, the historic homestead of George Washington, the nation's first president. There could hardly have been a darker, or more fitting omen, for the coming horror of the Civil War.

The dead soldiers were casualties from the battle at Ball's Bluff, a small but disastrous Union offensive on the town of Leesburg, 30 miles or so up the Potomac from Washington. From the beginning, it was unclear what, exactly, Union command hoped to accomplish by the assault. History tells us that the commanding officer of the Army of the Potomac, General McClellan, was uneasy about the

Confederate presence in Leesburg, Virginia, and sent orders out to Brigadier General Charles Stone to make a "slight demonstration" that might "have the effect of moving the Confederates" from their position. What this "slight demonstration" was, exactly, was left to the imagination of Brigadier General Stone, and so the Union general ordered his ill-fated amphibious assault across the Potomac River.

The attack commenced early in the morning of October 21, with Colonel Edward Baker leading a group of soldiers across the Potomac River under cover of darkness. Colonel Baker was one of the Union army's celebrity officers. Though he had almost no military experience to speak of, Baker earned his rank from his distinguished civilian career, having been an elected senator prior to the Civil War and a personal friend of Abraham Lincoln's. On orders from Stone, the celebrated, though untested, colonel led over 1000 men across the Potomac and up Ball's Bluff, a steep embankment looming over the Virginian side of the river.

Baker's landing on the southern bank was a rather chaotic affair, hamstrung by a shortage of boats and the hard ascent up Ball's Bluff. By the time the Union men were ready for the march on Leesburg, a Confederate force under the command of the battle-hardened Brigadier General Nathan Evans was ready to receive them. What followed was an unmitigated disaster for Baker and his men.

Evans, veteran of the First Battle of Manassas, commanded a force essentially equal in size to that of Colonel Baker's, but enjoyed the advantages of defense and a skilled body of soldiers under his command, advantages that he brought to good use soon after Baker's men crested Ball's Bluff. Baker's men had barely begun their advance towards Leesburg when they met determined Confederate resistance. The fight was fully joined soon after midday, with sharp fire being exchanged up and down the Confederate and Union lines. Under pressure of the Confederate attack, the Union advance halted, wavered and then began to fall back. The turning point came when Colonel Baker was shot off his horse by a Confederate sharpshooter early on in the fighting, killed in plain sight of most of his men. By 6 AM, the Union soldiers were on the verge of a panicked rout, pushed all the way back to the Potomac, their backs to Ball's Bluff's sheer drop, barely holding their wavering line together.

Recognizing that his adversaries were nearing their breaking point, Evans deemed it time to deliver the coup de grâce and ordered his men to charge. The shrill whoop of the rebel yell sounded over the battlefield, and all at once, over 1000 Southern men rushed towards the distraught Union soldiers teetering over the Potomac. That was it. Whatever resolve was left in the Northern ranks dissolved before the oncoming line of bayonets, and the thin blue line stretched along Ball's Bluff broke apart. The chaos of the last moments at Ball's Bluff was such that it resonated across the United States, a terrified tremor that spread from the shores of the Potomac to Washington, D.C., through the streets of New York and into the far-thest-flung Michigan backwoods.

Stuck between the oncoming Confederates and the steep drop into the Potomac, the Union soldiers had nowhere to go. Hundreds of them took the headlong

The Battle at Ball's Bluff was a devastating loss for the Union troops; the battlefield is said to be haunted by the fallen soldiers to this day.

plunge down Ball's Bluff, skidding and tumbling into the river, their enemies firing down at their backs as they ran. Many of the Union dead were picked up by the Potomac's current and carried downstream to Washington, D.C. As for those men who made their stand on the top of the bluff, they found it in themselves to continue the fight for another hour or so, before sudden and outright surrender. By eight o'clock that night, the Confederates were marching over 700 prisoners to Leesburg.

Brigadier General Stone's defeat at Ball's Bluff enraged the Northern public. While it was a relatively minor engagement compared to other Civil War battles, it had a major impact on popular perceptions of the war. Ball's Bluff followed close on the heels of the major Union defeat at the Battle of Bull Run, was a complete defeat at the hands of an equal foe, saw the loss of a prominent colonel and had its casualties float through the heart of the nation's capital. Someone had to take the fall for this terrible blunder.

The focus of the public's ire fell on General Charles Stone, the senior officer who ordered the advance over the Potomac. It didn't matter that the general wasn't on the battlefield and didn't give a single field command—the people needed a scapegoat, and Stone was offered up on the altar of public opinion. In the wake of the battle, Congress established the Congressional Joint Committee on the Conduct of War and promptly had General Stone arrested for what they called "the most atrocious blunder in history." Stone would spend over five months in prison, to be set free only when the furor over Ball's Bluff died down.

Though Stone was given a military commission after he was released from prison, for the rest of his life he would never be able to rid himself of the stigma of his failure at Ball's Bluff. It haunted him to his grave. As it turned out, he wasn't the only one haunted by it. The Ball's Bluff National Cemetery was established shortly after the war, in December 1865. With a mere 54 Union casualties buried there, it was, and remains, the United States' smallest military cemetery. But what it lacks in size, it has certainly made up for in infamy.

Stories of strange goings-on in the cemetery surrounding the battlefield began circulating not long after the first visitors came and went. It is impossible to say who experienced them first—the disembodied shouts in the darkness, the painful wails, the battle cries, the faint shimmering apparitions running towards Ball's Bluff. Year after year, people continued to hear and see these phenomena. Of course, there was little question about the origin of these sights and sounds. People were quick to point out the misguided Union offensive and ultimately vain sacrifices of the soldiers buried in the cemetery. Could the spirits of these men be as angry about the loss at Ball's Bluff as the public was? Were their appearances at the National Cemetery an expression of the trauma of their last moments, their ire at having given up their lives for naught?

If so, there is reason to believe the spirits there are still fixated on their untimely deaths. For even to this day, almost 150 years after the battle, the ghosts of Ball's Bluff are said to haunt the field where they fell. Indeed, the many inexplicable encounters over the years have made the Civil War battlefield into something of a supernatural landmark. The stories have been repeated so many times that most residents of Loudoun County near Ball's Bluff barely give them a second thought. Or the adults don't, anyway. Among local teenagers, however, the Civil War ghosts are still something of an attraction.

In the 1950s, Loudoun County kids took to driving out to the battlefield at night, looking for thrills. These weekend excursions were usually nothing more than excuses for teenagers to get the lead out, and any Civil War ghosts hoping to be noticed would have to make a lot of noise over the

Creating a ghastly flotilla, bodies of soldiers killed at Ball's Bluff floated down the Potomac River all the way to Washington, D.C.

rambunctious, often semi-inebriated cavorting. Yet while the teenagers were able to shout out the ghosts more often than not, enough nocturnal forays ended in supernatural encounters that the legend of Ball's Bluff was kept alive.

The ghosts usually make their entrance with a cacophony of screams, shouts and painful wails along with the rumble of rifle fire and cannon—distant at first, faint, and then growing clearer, until the darkness is alive with the sounds of anachronistic battle, causing bushes to tremble and boughs to shake. That is when a sudden chill descends over the area, and vague outlines of soldiers are seen darting around the cemetery, moving to the direction of unheard commands. We might imagine the reaction of teenagers as the ghosts emerge from the night, waging their supernatural battle all around them. Some witnesses stay longer than others, but all end up running for their cars, getting away as fast as possible.

It is at this point that the spirits of Ball's Bluff demonstrate the full extent of their power. Cars revved into a hasty escape have been held in place by some invisible and unyielding force. Tires spin and engines whine, but the vehicles remain stationary, straining against the inhuman strength until they are abruptly released after about half a minute, sent roaring away from the cursed battlefield. Evidence of the encounter is always the same, visible when the frightened teenagers feel they are far enough away to stop their car, step out and look for any damage. They are there every time, year after year—two enormous handprints of muddy clay, planted on the back of the car.

The ghosts at Ball's Bluff have been expressing their aversion to automobiles since the 1950s, and given the stories that continue to circulate, the dead soldiers share the same dislike for 2003 Honda Civics as they did for '57 Chevys. We can only guess why the ghosts of Ball's Bluff have remained behind, and why they continue to relive their battle before the terrified eyes of curious teenagers. Maybe they have lost all concept of the passage of time and keep fighting over Ball's Bluff because they have never been able to get over the terror of their final moments. Or perhaps they remain behind in their hope to impart some lesson of the horror and futility of war. Whether their spirits are possessed by a mission or possessed by an unmitigated madness, their lingering presence has succeeded in keeping the country's smallest national cemetery on the map, and ensuring that their sacrifice is not forgotten.

The Hessians at Buttonwood

General Knyphausen's Hessians were flush with the joy of victory. The Battle of Brandywine had come at a high price, the dead and wounded numbering nearly 2000. But those who had weathered the battle embraced life after it with the zeal of the professional soldier. Survival was the preeminent virtue among many of the Hessians fighting on American soil, and they made it a habit to celebrate it heartily.

Two such Brandywine survivors stumbled onto the Buttonwood House on their way to Philadelphia. They were Hessian jaegers, serving as advance scouts for Knyphausen's force miles ahead of the advancing column. Their hearts jumped when they caught sight of the solitary house in the woods. A sturdy stone building, already close to a century old in 1777, the house looked warm and inviting in the cold fall twilight, and the two soldiers stared covetously at the golden firelight radiating from the windows. Dreams of full steins of pilsner and roast boar danced through their minds. And wasn't this their right? After all, they were marching through the enemy's territory after having just defeated its army. Wasn't this house, along with everything inside it, fair game? Both men had survived the close and vicious fighting at Brandywine. Wouldn't there be any spoils for their efforts? Of course there would be, they thought as they peered at the stone house through the darkening woods. This house would be their prize.

The two Hessians fastened their bayonets to their rifles and put on their fiercest faces, steeling themselves for whatever waited inside. Neither man could have possibly known it when they barged into the old stone house, but it turned out that their fiercest faces weren't fierce enough for the danger that awaited them in Buttonwood House, which wasn't nearly as inviting as it looked from the outside.

"Achtung!" came the shout just before they kicked open the front door and rushed inside, the tips of their rifles leading the way. At first sight, it was everything they might have wished for. The air in the house was close and warm, saturated with the smell of spices that came from a cauldron of bubbling rabbit stew. A rough-hewn wood table in the center of the main room was loaded with bread, cheese, a knife and a big wooden cask of home brew. The half-emptied flagon of dark frothy ale next to the bread and cheese gave away the cask's contents. All the scene lacked was a pair of smiling *fräuleins* willing to serve the feast up.

Instead they faced a burly Pennsylvanian yeoman, startled from his early evening feast by the soldiers' forceful entry, and looking none too happy about it either; the man's wife stood behind him, her arms wrapped around two children—a girl and a boy. The Hessians did not speak English and so resorted to getting their point across by barking monosyllabic orders and jutting their rifles towards the family members when they needed to emphasize a point. Before long, the soldiers had herded the family into a corner of the stone house and were sitting at the dinner table, making themselves at home with the dinner that had been prepared.

Things would have ended differently if the Hessians had left it at that. But after they finished the stew and a few cups

of beer, they began going through the Pennsylvanians'
belongings, looking for anything that might be of value.
That was when the man of the house decided to do something about these two looters. "You've eaten your fill," the
man hollered, stepping away from the corner of the room,
"but that's all ye'll take from this house!"

"Halt!" screamed one of the soldiers, thrusting his bayonet towards the advancing man.

"*Züruck Gleiben!*" shouted the other, striding forward.

"I said, get out of my house!" came the Pennsylvanian's
response, as he walked a few more paces until he stood
face-to-face with the closest intruder.

Neither party understood the other, but everyone in
the house could sense where the standoff was going. The
Hessian standing in front of the Pennsylvanian made the
first move, jamming his rifle across his adversary's chest
in an attempt to get the man at rifle's length and within
striking distance. The owner of Buttonwood moved
quickly, grabbing the Hessian's rifle by the barrel with
both hands and yanking hard. Caught completely by surprise by this bold move, the Hessian lost his grip on his
weapon and tumbled forward into the now-armed
Pennsylvanian. The other soldier shouted in alarm and
raised his rifle to his shoulder a split-second ahead of his
target, who sidestepped the falling soldier in front of him
and leveled his recently acquired rifle at the armed
Hessian. For a instant, both men stood with loaded guns
pointed at one another, no more than 7 feet apart.

When the man's daughter screamed, both men fired.
Their shots went off almost simultaneously—two muzzle
flashes and two bursts of gun smoke, which quickly

spread through the room. But only one man was hit. *"Mein Gott"* came the weak moan from within the smoke-filled room. The Hessian clutched the gaping wound in his chest, wheezing his last breaths through his bleeding lungs as the man who killed him promptly fell into a life-or-death struggle with the remaining soldier.

Just before he fired, the American had fallen to one knee, effectively dodging the Hessian's fire while keeping his foe in his sights. He pulled the trigger a blink after the German soldier had, but his aim was true, and the soldier fell to the ground, mortally wounded. The first Hessian had been dealt with, but the second now lunged, knocking the Pennsylvanian prone, leaping atop him and wrapping his hands around the man's throat. The Buttonwood resident was helpless under the weight of the Hessian, and his strength was fading rapidly as the soldier tightened his grip around his windpipe. In one final bid for survival, he reached up to the tabletop, his hands grasping for anything he might use as a weapon. His grip found the handle of his kitchen knife and brought it down on the Hessian with all the strength he could muster, embedding the utensil in the side of the soldier's throat and sending him into his gurgling death throes.

The smoke cleared on a gory scene in Buttonwood's main room. Two blood-soaked Hessians lay on the floor. Unhurt, the Pennsylvanian regained his feet, his glance going from the two mortally wounded Hessians to where his family was huddled. He knew that an army of men would be close behind these two scouts, and he was seized by the immediate importance of disposing of the bodies. If he took them outside to bury them he would risk being spotted by other scouts that might be scouring the area. Deciding he would have to hide the bodies in his house until the Hessian army passed by, he got to work cleaning the blood off the floor and then dragged the two men into the attic.

The Pennsylvanian managed to clean up the blood before the rest of the Hessians arrived the next morning. Unlike the two scouts who came the night before, these soldiers were in the company of their commanding officer and were much better behaved. It is said that General Knyphausen himself visited the Buttonwood House, courteously asking the American family about the local terrain and foraging prospects, unaware that two of his soldiers lay dead in the attic. And so it was that the family living in Buttonwood narrowly dodged the wrath of the invading army. For three days and three nights, the dead Hessians remained in the Buttonwood attic, to be dragged out to the woods and buried only when the man who killed them was certain all of Knyphausen's soldiers had passed. No one knows where, exactly, the Pennsylvanian dug their graves, but if one is to believe all the tales that came out of Buttonwood in the following years, their spirits did not go very far.

Buttonwood became a topic of discussion among Chester County residents soon after the War of Independence had ended. People spoke in hushed tones about the queer goings-on in the old stone house. The rumors began with isolated incidents. A traveler walking by Buttonwood would swear to have spied two deathly pale faces staring down from the attic window. Some claimed to have seen two transparent men dressed in the green coats and white breeches of the Hessian soldiers creeping through the woods surrounding the house. Visitors to the stone house talked about lively dinner conversations abruptly interrupted by the sounds of angry footsteps from above, causing the home's inhabitants to blanch in fear, holding their breath until the pacing stopped.

The years brought more accounts. Subsequent owners of Buttonwood spoke of the dark bloodstain on the attic floor that did not wash away, no matter how hard they scrubbed. And just like this stain, neither did the Hessian apparitions fade, even as the war that claimed their lives receded ever further into the past. In fact, if anything, the apparitions seemed to grow more corporeal with the passing years, appearing with greater frequency, eliciting a more profound and lasting terror when spotted. Accounts of the Hessians grew so common in the decades following the Revolutionary War that Buttonwood acquired a rather morbid reputation during the first half of the 19th century.

Then the Civil War broke out. The moment the Southern states announced their secession from the Union, locals stopped seeing the Hessians. We can only guess why. Perhaps the great tragedy of the war looming imminently on the horizon somehow pushed the spirits of past confrontations off the paranormal landscape. Is there room for only so many ghosts, only so much misery, in any region's supernatural register? Could it be that the lingering spirits of past wars were ushered out of Chester County in preparation for the flood of incoming dead that fell on Civil War battlefields? Or maybe it was a matter of comparison. What fear or awe could the spirits of two creeping Hessians awake in the hearts of people who, day to day, were coping with the very real terror of a war that was upending their world?

Though these theories might shed light on why the Hessians' spirits faded from Buttonwood, they don't explain why they came back. It cannot be said for certain when, exactly, they came back, but reports of the Hessians at Buttonwood started to circulate again sometime in the 1950s. While the house's inhabitants haven't had much to say about the purported hauntings, the story has come to life among a few local ghost enthusiasts and curiosity seekers, who eagerly grasp at any rumors of Hessian sightings. And according to some, the sightings still occur. Appearing as exaggerated anachronisms that wander around the house they were killed in, the Hessians still appear in their traditional dress—their green coats and white pants, pale as the ghosts they are—sulking around Buttonwood, perhaps looking for the bounty that evaded them so long ago.

The End

GHOST HOUSE

GHOST HOUSE BOOKS

Add to your ghost house collection with these books full of fascinating mysteries and terrifying tales.

NEW MAY 2004
Urban Legends *by A.S. Mott*

This book collects many of the intriguing modern myths that persistently do the rounds at water coolers all over the nation, from the vanishing hitchhiker to the tarantula crawling out of the bananas at the local grocery store. Great fun— you'll likely recognize a tale or two you've told friends yourself!
$10.95USD/$14.95CDN • ISBN 1-894877-41-1 • 5.25" x 8.25" • 232 pages

NEW JUNE 2004
Victorian Ghost Stories *by Jo-Anne Christensen*

The Victorian era was a golden age of the paranormal. Famous writers, such as Charles Dickens and Edgar Allan Poe, created fantastic tales that remain the models for contemporary ghost stories. As the interest in the paranormal grew, body snatchers stole corpses from cemeteries and scientists tried to reanimate them, reflecting a society on the brink of madness. Join best-selling author Jo-Anne Christensen as she explores the most bizarre and remarkable stories from this fascinating era of haunted history.
$10.95USD/$14.95CDN • ISBN 1-894877-35-7 • 5.25" x 8.25" • 240 pages

NEW AUGUST 2004
Haunted Cemeteries *by Edrick Thay*

Cemeteries are supposed to be places of quiet repose, where the dead are left to their eternal rest. Some spirits, however, just can't sleep. Edrick Thay shares eyewitness accounts set in graveyards around the world, including the vampire-plagued Highgate Cemetery in London and Egypt's ancient Valley of the Kings.
$10.95USD/$14.95CDN • ISBN 1-894877-60-8 • 5.25" x 8.25" • 216 pages

These and many more Ghost House books are available from
your local bookseller or by ordering direct.
U.S. readers call 1-800-518-3541. In Canada, call 1-800-661-9017.